The Inverness and Ross-shire Railway

The railway from Inverness to Bonar Bridge

Keith Fe[illegible]

Published by
the Highland Railway Society
to mark the
150th anniversary of
the opening of the line between
Inverness and Dingwall

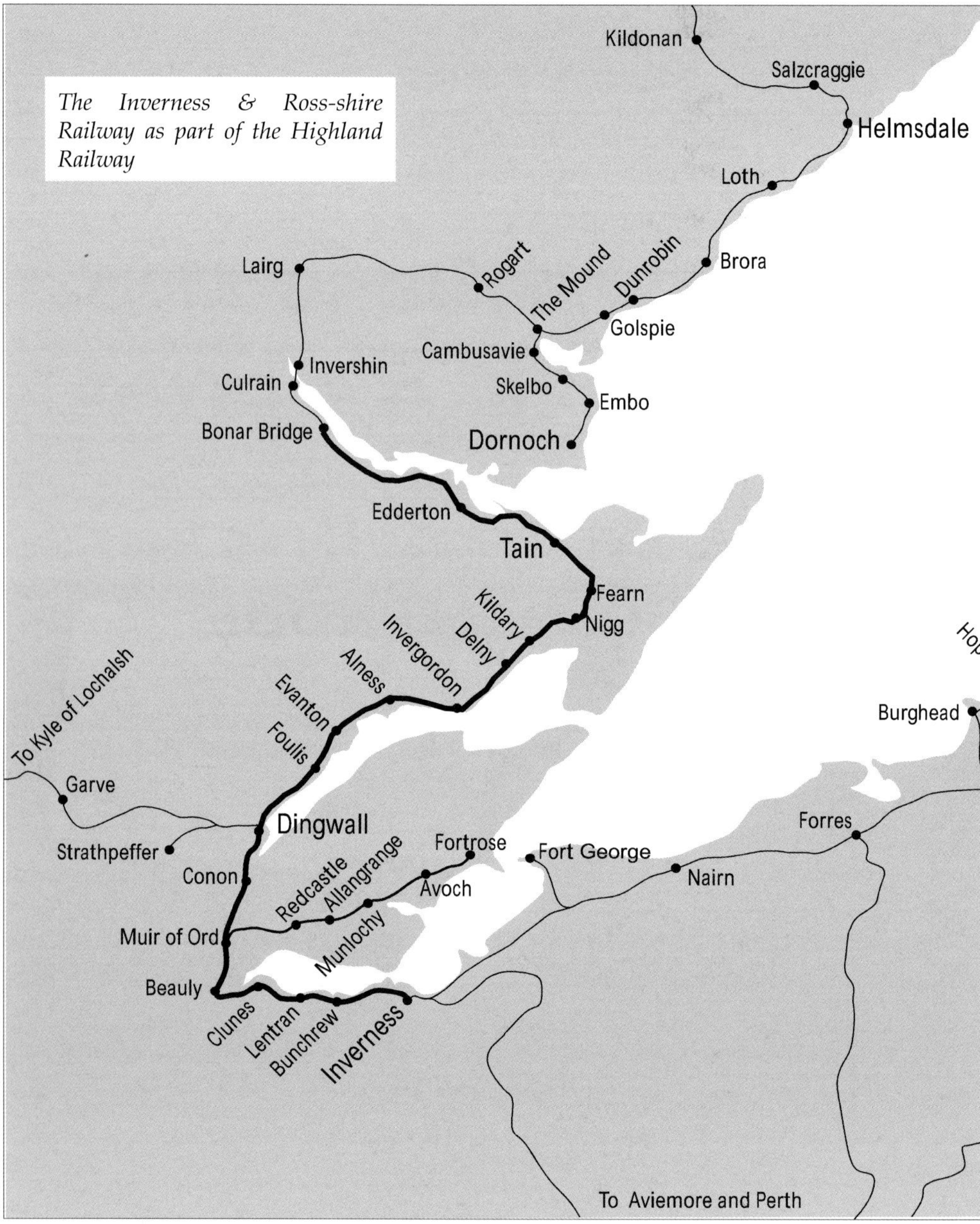

ISBN: 978 0 95454857 5

Published by the Highland Railway Society : www.hrsoc.org.uk.

Printed by Henry Ling Ltd, Dorchester

Contents

Acronyms

GNSR	Great North of Scotland Railway
I&AJ	Inverness & Aberdeen Junction Railway
I&N	Inverness & Nairn Railway
I&PJ	Inverness & Perth Junction Railway
I&RR	Inverness & Ross-shire Railway

Front Cover : a northbound train composed of two Class 156 diesel multiple units waits to leave Dingwall for the north in August 1989. At that time, trains were not running between Dingwall and Inverness due to the collapse of the Ness bridge. Buses conveyed passengers. The van on the platform, from Sharp's Reliable Wrecks, carried passengers' heavy luggage and bicycles. The train was in British Railways' Regional Railways sector livery. It would split at Georgemas so that both Wick and Thurso were served directly, unlike present day practice where the train serves Thurso and then Wick. The goods sidings and goods shed can be seen behind the train, but by then they were out of use. A Class 37 loco occupied one of the sidings. *(Keith Fenwick)*

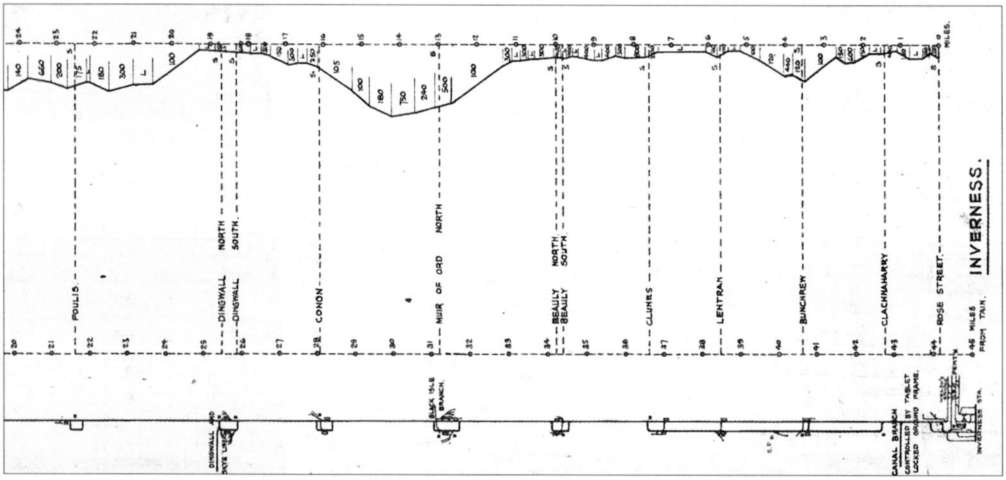

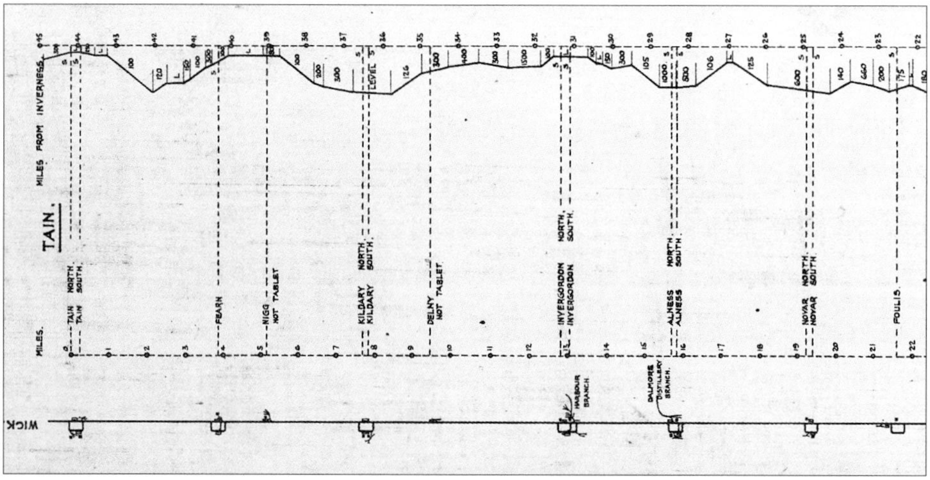

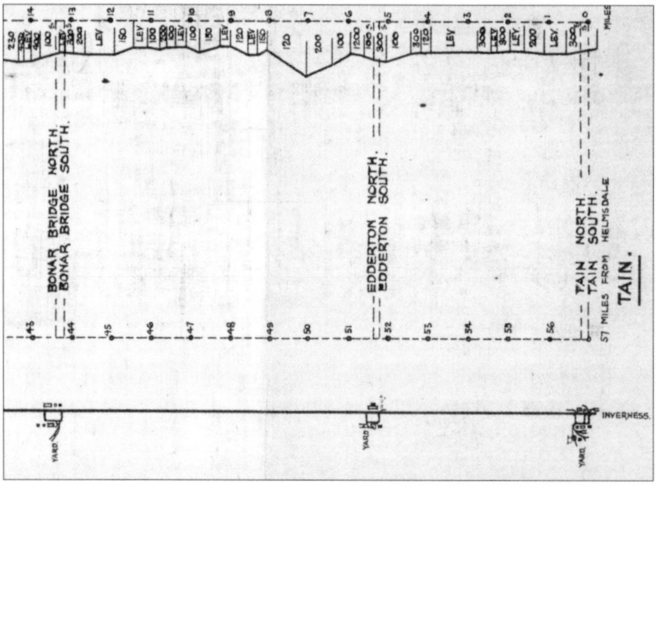

These charts of the line date from LMS days. They show all the signal boxes, track layouts in basic form and, on the right, gradients. One chart covered Helmsdale to Tain, from which the section above is taken. Another covered Tain to Inverness (here split to fit on the page).

Introduction

Inverness, the capital of the Highlands, was an independent town. The leading lights were the local lairds and clan chiefs and it was their determination to promote the prosperity of the town which influenced the development of railways in the region. They were also the source of finance for railway construction. Initially this spirit of independence actually delayed building the first railway to the town but in due course the Highland Railway was established with its centre at Inverness and connections north, south, east and west.

The coming of railways to the Highlands actually followed quite soon after proper roads were built. Under the auspices of the Commissioners of Highland Roads and Bridges, a road network was established in the 1820s and 30s and this enabled coach routes to be started. Steamer services were also introduced in this period, but mainly on the west coast. Inverness was linked to the south via the Caledonian Canal. Several attempts were made to run similar services along the east coast but winter weather and exposed harbours limited their effectiveness. The advantages of better communication were therefore already apparent to those in the northern counties when railways started spreading throughout the country.

The first serious proposals were made in 1845, at the height of the railway mania. A direct line over the hills to Perth and a more easily graded line, the Great North of Scotland, from Aberdeen were both proposed but it was the latter which was authorised in 1846. By then the railway mania was over and finance was hard to find. As the GNSR was controlled by Aberdeen commercial interests it did not receive any support from Inverness; with their backing construction could have started much sooner. It was not until the early 1850s that the GNSR had started building from the Aberdeen end but it was clearly not going to complete its line throughout, so the Inverness parties began construction from the northern end with the Inverness & Nairn Railway and this opened in 1856. Completion of the through route was achieved by the Inverness & Aberdeen Junction Railway, promoted by those same Inverness interests, in 1858.

As the larger company, the I&AJ took over operation of the I&N and then absorbed it in 1861. By that time, construction had started on the line over the hills to Perth by the Inverness & Perth Junction Railway. Again, this was operated by the I&AJ after its opening in 1863 and the two companies amalgamated to form the Highland Railway in 1865.

Before that happened, extension of the railway system north of Inverness was underway. Much of the route was obvious, along the east coast where the population was concentrated to reach the final objective of Wick and Thurso. But while the distance as the crow flies was 80 miles, by rail as built it was twice that. A shorter route could have been taken but that would have involved expensive bridges beyond the engineering capabilities of the time; it has never been justified as an improvement since then. Even financing the easier coastal route presented a serious challenge. Great economy had to be practised in construction and the line was built in stages. It seems quite remarkable, therefore, that it only took fifteen years from the first steps being taken to completion to Wick.

In this book, we look at the construction of the southern part of the line as far as Bonar Bridge. From Inverness, it was opened in stages: to Dingwall in 1862, Invergordon the following year and Bonar Bridge in 1864. As far as Invergordon, the line was promoted as the Inverness & Ross-shire Railway, an offshoot of the Inverness & Aberdeen Junction Railway, but the latter took it over in 1862 and built the section to Bonar Bridge. The promotion of a separate company ensured that the capital could be raised from those who would be served by the line and therefore benefit from it rather than shareholders in existing lines. Prominent among the shareholders was the Duke of Sutherland. He used his great wealth, derived from the collieries of Staffordshire, to support railway development into the county of Sutherland.

The graceful lines of the Ness Viaduct are shown in this early view taken downstream on the west bank. The quay is out of view to the left on the far bank. *(HRS/Roberts collection)*

One pier remained after the floods of 1989 destroyed the Ness Viaduct and the track was left hanging between the two sides of the river. These remains had to be removed before the new bridge could be constructed. *(J L Stevenson)*

Promotion of the Line

The first steps towards railway extension north of Inverness were taken in January 1859. To put this in context, the through route from Aberdeen had only been open for a few months and promotion of the direct line south to Perth had not started. At that time a railway was not seen as the solution by everyone. The time taken by sea from the Moray coast to Easter Ross compared favourably with that by the long rail route via Inverness. The Duke of Sutherland funded the development of the port at Littleferry so that a service could run from there to Burghead for connections to the south via Aberdeen; this was operating three times a week in 1855. But coastal shipping was handicapped by winter conditions. A writer to the *Inverness Courier* in December 1855 suggested that services could be "entirely suspended for several days when the easterly winds raise the German ocean into one plane of moveable mountains, in successive barriers, stretching across from the Sutherland side to the Moray side of the Firth." It was not difficult to see why support for the railway grew. The service to Littleferry continued until the mid-1860s, but once the railway was opened north from Inverness it disappeared.

A meeting was held on 18th January 1859 at the Union Hotel, Inverness, to consider the practicality and expediency of constructing a Railway from Inverness to Dingwall via Beauly. Present were several directors of the I&AJ, together with owners through whose land the line would pass, such as Lord Lovat. Joseph Mitchell, who had made his name working for the Commission for Highland Roads and Bridges and then turned his attention to railway promotion in the north, outlined the route of the line and showed how it was an extension of the I&N and I&AJ. He had clearly thought through the questionable financial prospects of the line when he stated that "unless the proprietors along the line were prepared to have their land valued at a moderate annual agricultural value and to capitalise that value by the applications of a moderate multiple and to invest that capital ... in the stock of the line, the railway could not be made."

Donald Matheson, on behalf of the I&AJ, wished every possible success to the new undertaking. When the line was completed, the I&AJ would be very glad to work it in as cheap a manner as they could. They would be happy to promote it in every way they could, but at that time it was not in their power to make any advances towards the capital cost. The meeting agreed that a committee be formed to promote the undertaking and canvas for support. Mitchell was instructed to carry out a survey.

Progress over the next few months seems to have been quite slow. A meeting in May noted that only 15 positive replies had been received but a prospectus was commissioned. In August, Mitchell informed the committee that the estimated cost of line was £135,059. He stated that the line would be remunerative given the traffic on lines already made in this locality. He suggested that the contractors might take £30,000 of stock, leaving £60,000 for shareholders to find after the parliamentary deposit had been raised. Lovat was asked to convene a meeting of landowners to consider the price and value of their land.

Meetings now became more frequent as the necessary steps towards promotion of the Bill were taken. Various subscriptions for shares were considered at the end of August and in early

September draft agreements with landowners considered. Terms under which the I&AJ would operate the line were also discussed; this was provisionally set at 50% of gross receipts.

Later in September, a public meeting was held at Inverness Castle, attended by 35 people, including the committee, Mitchell etc. Resolutions were carried stating that the extension of railway communication northwards from Inverness was essential and that the extension was of great importance to Inverness trade and commerce and the prospective increase of the Town. Another resolution supported the view "that the success which has attended Railway enterprise between Aberdeen and Inverness [is] an answered guarantee for the prospects of its extension northwards in communication with existing lines."

Continuing the line on to Invergordon was now being actively discussed and it was for this longer line that the Prospectus was issued in November 1859 and a Bill submitted to Parliament under the title Inverness & Ross-shire Railway. The initial list of directors included two each from the I&N and I&AJ as both these companies agreed to take shares in the Ross-shire. The Bill initially faced opposition from the Magistrates and Town Council of Dingwall over provisions for crossing the Dingwall Canal and the protection of Dingwall Harbour. This was settled by making this a swing bridge if required by the Council and so the Bill had a smooth passage through Parliament and received Royal Assent on 3rd July 1860. As well as incorporating the Company, it authorised raising capital of £215,000 with the usual power to borrow a third of that in addition, i.e. £71,600. The I&AJ could subscribe £15,000 and the I&N £10,000 and either of these companies could work the line. The Company was obliged to extend the 'new wooden quay' at Inverness by a distance of 108 yards outwards and dredge in front of the quay. The line had to start at the I&N station at Inverness and a branch to the Caledonian Canal at Muirtown basin was included. The opening bridge over the Caledonian Canal at Clachnaharry had to be made to the satisfaction of the Canal Commissioners. The railway had to be completed within five years .

While the Bill was being considered in Parliament, the construction contractor was selected. The works were not onerous except that there were three major river bridges, at Inverness, Beauly and Conon. The plans were only complete as far as Dingwall, so that contract was let first. Tenders were considered in June, 1860. Mitchell had estimated the cost at £84,156 9s 8d; the lowest tender was £79,054 plus £450 for maintenance for 6 months; the most expensive was £118,500. The one selected was from Meakin of Birkenhead at £80,454 including a stone bridge over the River Ness, plus £900 for maintenance for the first six months after opening. Meakin was the only contractor with named securities; Mitchell advised that it was desirable that the Contractor had "... not only ample capital, but great experience, energy and skill to apply to the crossing of the Ness, the Beauly and the Conon. I am of the opinion that Mr Meakin should be preferred to the Contract."

Building the Line

At the first meeting of the company after the passing of the Act, Andrew Dougall, Manager of the I&N and I&AJ Railways, was appointed to also manage the Ross-shire. This cemented the close relationship between the three companies. It was reported that the contract for construction to Dingwall had been let at £80,454 with a further £26,000 for permanent way. A further £9,500 was required to cross the Caledonian Canal and provide station houses.

The first sod was cut on 19th September 1860 by Mrs Matheson, wife of the chairman. The day was observed as a general holiday in Inverness. At 3pm, a procession headed by the militia started for the field situated opposite the "White House" on the outskirts of the city, where Mr Meakin, the contractor, was waiting. After the first sod was cut with due ceremony, the party returned to the town and in the evening the directors were entertained to dinner. The following day the *Inverness Courier* reported that "This line, we may remind our readers, is the next great step in the progress of railway communication northwards. There are several heavy works on the line, but, as a whole, it is easy of construction; favourable arrangements have been made with landowners, the contract price is moderate, and the shareholders are sanguine that this will be one of the best paying railway undertakings in the North. The cost of construction is about £7,000 per mile."

Construction proceeded during the next few months, with the objective of opening the following year. The Minutes do not give much information on progress, but expenditure seems to have been a concern in March 1861, when Matheson proposed a resolution that was approved unanimously: "The Board being desirous of ensuring the strictest economy in the construction of the Line and being strongly of opinion that the ultimate success of the Lines in the North, where the Country is thinly populated and great competition for the traffic exists by sea, depends very much on the amount of the original cost, it was resolved that no deviation from Plans or Contracts involving extra expenditure of money, however small, be entered into without obtaining the express sanction of the Board by a minute…" It went on to set other conditions, including the importance of opening in 1861 and that "all the stations on the line to be constructed of timber and in the most economical manner."

Later that month, five tenders for the line from Dingwall to Invergordon were considered, ranging from £45,952 13s 0d to £51,500. The lowest was MacDonald and Grieve of Granton and that was accepted after "satisfactory enquiries" had been made.

This was, of course, the period of maximum expenditure and the Board had to juggle outgoings with the available capital. Not all shares had been taken up and subscriptions were paid in instalments, or calls. To get over a cash flow problem, a loan of £20,000 was arranged with the Caledonian Bank in April.

The half yearly meeting on 30th April 1861 heard that satisfactory progress was being made in construction considering the severe weather of the previous winter. Permanent way had been laid down in many places and the majority of the smaller bridges built. The Conon bridge had made good progress and the wooden bridge at Beauly would be complete in a few months. Difficulty had been experienced in getting a good foundation for the Ness viaduct; the abutment and one pier were now beyond the influence of water and the rest should soon

A wooden bridge was built over the River Beauly for the opening of the line. It was 460 feet long between abutments and had eight openings of 35 feet span and nine openings of 20 feet span. East of that there was another viaduct of similar construction with 200 feet span, having ten 20 feet openings, for the passage of flood water. In 1881 a single steel span built by Head Wrightson was installed at the east end of the main bridge. The photograph above shows it in this condition. The remaining wooden sections were replaced by a steel structure supported on stone piers in 1909 as shown in the photograph below. After this was taken, the 1881 span in the foreground was replaced.

(Above John Roake collection, below HRS/Roberts collection)

be secured. There was a suggestion that the line might be open as far as Dingwall once that section was complete, but it would be advantageous to open the whole line at the same time.

In June, the Admiralty wrote to state they had not approved the bridge over the Ness and required an opening span of 40 feet; the Harbour trustees however considered the bridge was sufficient. The Company was able to prevent the Admiralty getting an interdict to stop the work but the following month the Admiralty changed its mind and suggested a flat iron bridge to withstand floods. As it turned out, the stone bridge was destroyed by floods, but not until 1989. After the line was opened, items used in the construction of the bridge were offered for sale; these included two piling engines with portable boiler on wheels, cast iron rams and two 18-inch cast iron pumps. These were to 'be sold at a bargain' so possibly the cost of transporting them for use elsewhere reduced their value.

By October, over half the capital had been expended, so the company was in a position to exercise its borrowing powers, although some creative accounting may have been used as all shares should have been issued and this was not the case.

By that time amalgamation of the I&N and the I&AJ had taken place and amalgamation of the I&RR was being discussed in detail. This would obviate the need for a working agreement and simplify the management and accounting.

The agreed terms of amalgamation set the capital of the I&RR at £245,000 on which £83,000 had been paid and that of the I&AJ as £675,000 of which £560,000 was subscribed. I&RR shares that were paid up at the amalgamation were to be converted into a 3% stock which would rise ½% per year until the dividend matched the I&AJ ordinary dividend, when the stocks would be merged. Both companies would promote an amalgamation Bill in the 1862 session "and every session thereafter" until an Act was obtained.

Meanwhile, all hope of opening in 1861 had vanished and construction continued into 1862. In the middle of March, Mitchell reported that the section to Dingwall was expected to open later the following month; the half-yearly meeting on 23rd April was told the works had made great progress in the previous six months and that it was now hoped to open in about two weeks. The contractors were under penalty to have it open by 12th August.

Even so, it was not until 10th June that Major Yolland carried out the statutory Board of Trade Inspection of the section to Dingwall. He reported that the line, 18 miles 33 chains, ran into a separate platform at Inverness station but a short junction line had been constructed to join the I&AJ and the junctions were protected by signals. The line was single throughout with a through siding and passing place at Beauly station; over and under bridges were constructed and land bought for single line only. There were stations on the line at Bunchrew, Lentran, Beauly, Tarradale, Conon and Dingwall. There was an engine turntable at Inverness and a turntable at Dingwall on which engines could be turned when separated from their tenders, and the Company had engaged not to run with the tender forward. To better improve safety to the public, the Engineer had undertaken that at the junction at Inverness the new method of partially connecting the signals and points was to be introduced without delay; and at the swing bridge over the Caledonian Canal mechanical means were to be introduced by which the signalman would be prevented from lowering the signal for the passage of a train until the bridge was fixed in the proper position for it to pass over. As a result he recommended that the line could open.

The Directors, several of whom had been in the inspection party, decided to open the line the following day. Dougall telegraphed from Dingwall to Inverness to order all the officials to leave that evening by special train and to be set down at their respective posts. Large placards

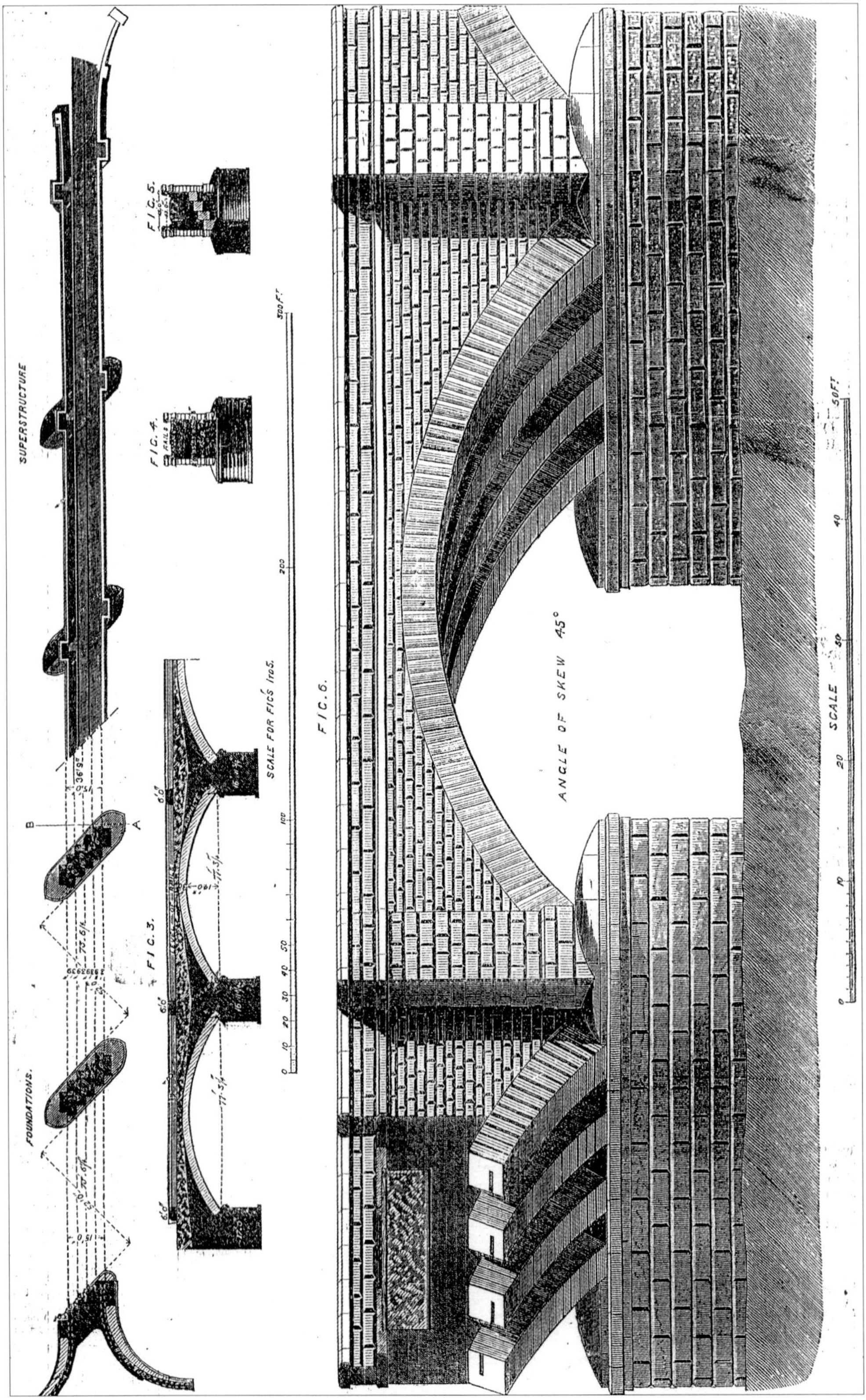
SUPERSTRUCTURE
FOUNDATIONS.
FIG. 3.
FIG. 4.
FIG. 5.
SCALE FOR FIGS 1 TO 5.
FIG. 6.
ANGLE OF SKEW 45°
SCALE
50 FT

announcing the opening were posted on the walls of the town by 5pm and trains started on Wednesday 11th June.

Four trains ran each way and traffic on the first day was quite heavy, partly because Muir of Ord market was in progress. Sheep and cattle from the north arrived by several trains. A celebratory dinner was held at the National Hotel at Dingwall the following evening.

The Inverness holiday on 23rd July gave Invernessians their first real chance to travel over the new line; a total of 117 First class and 874 Third class tickets were issued from Inverness. Most people travelled all the way to Dingwall, of whom many went on by various conveyances or on foot to Strathpeffer which had never been so busy. Inns were full and a Frenchman there with an organ had a crowd around him. The final train back from Dingwall consisted of 7 First class carriages and 25 Thirds, 32 in all, hauled by two engines and even then "the speed was by no means great".

The Amalgamation Act came into effect on 30th June 1862, in reality a straight takeover by the I&AJ. Dividends on the Ross-shire shares did rise for the first two years and then 4% was paid on them until the financial crisis of 1866, after which they were much reduced.

Progress on the extension to Invergordon was slow. The keystone of the bridge at Alness was laid by Master Kenneth Matheson, the young laird of Ardross, in a ceremony on 10th August. That month, it was agreed that the station at Fowlis (as then spelt) was to be similar to the one at Bunchrew and those at Novar and Alness similar to Lentran. The Engineer was authorised to construct them of stone if he could do so and provide accommodation for the station master above the offices at an expense not exceeding £200 above the cost of a wooden structure. Fortunately stone buildings were erected.

Optimistic forecasts of the opening of the line continued to be made. At the half-yearly meeting in October 1862 opening by Christmas was predicted. One reason given was unforeseen difficulties in completing the works a little to the north of Dingwall. In fact this was a dispute with a local landowner, Mr MacKenzie of Findon, who demanded a bridge where Ferry Road

A substantial bridge was required at Conon with skewed arches. The view above looking downstream shows the road bridge in the distance while the design detail opposite shows how the complex skewed arches were constructed. *(Highland Railway Society)*

crossed the line because of the danger to his tenants if they had to use the proposed level crossing. A lightweight lattice bridge was put up in the end.

The line was finally ready for its inspection on 20th March 1863. The Inspector noted that there were crossing places at Dingwall and Novar and a short turntable at Invergordon which was to be used until the line was extended. Train control was by electric telegraph but he strongly recommended the Train Staff system; it would be nearly 30 years before token working was introduced.

As with the section to Dingwall, the line was quickly opened. The station masters, pointsmen and porters, "all skilled men", took up their respective places, fully equipped, on Saturday afternoon, and the line opened to traffic on Monday 23rd March 1863. The trains running to Dingwall were simply extended northwards but so little notice was given that there was little public recognition and not a single cheer for the first train when it arrived at Invergordon at 10.10am, although the station there was elaborately decorated with evergreens. A group of directors arrived on the second train and a luncheon was held for the principle residents of the town at 1pm. The *Inverness Courier* noted that there was little for the women who had come to the town with them to do; there was no room for them at the luncheon and they were left to wander about the town until the time of the return train.

INVERNESS AND ABERDEEN JUNCTION RAILWAY.

INVERNESS ANNUAL HOLIDAY.

SPECIAL TRAIN TO ABERDEEN, &c., AT 5 A.M.—
Fares—First Class, 11s. 3d. ; Third do., 7s. 6d.

CHEAP EXCURSION FARES
TO DINGWALL, BEAULY, NAIRN, FORRES, ELGIN, KEITH, BANFF, ABERDEEN, &c., &c.

ON *Wednesday, the 23d July* 1862, EXCURSION TICKETS will be issued at the INVERNESS STATION by the undernoted Trains, available to Return any day up to and including FRIDAY, the 25th July, by the Ordinary Passenger Trains, but not by Special Mail Trains on Great North Line, viz. :—To Portsoy, Banff, Huntly, Inveramsay, Inverury, Kintore, Aberdeen, by SPECIAL TRAIN from INVERNESS STATION at 5 A.M., arriving in Keith in time to be taken on by the Ordinary Passenger Train at 7 A.M., arriving in Aberdeen at 9·45 A.M., and return at 4·50 P.M., arriving in Inverness at 10·15 P.M. Excursionists will thus have upwards of 7 hours in Aberdeen.

To NAIRN, FORRES, ELGIN, FOCHABERS, and KEITH, and all Intermediate Stations, and also to the above-named Stations on the Banff, Portsoy, and Strathisla, and Great North of Scotland Railways, by the 6·40 A.M. and 10·5 A.M. Trains;

And to DINGWALL and BEAULY, and other Stations on Ross-shire Line, by the 8·20 and 10·30 A.M. Trains.

FARES FOR THE DOUBLE JOURNEY.

Between Inverness and	1st Class.	3d Class.	Between Inverness and	1st Class.	3d Class.
Dingwall	2s. 3d.	1s. 6d.	Elgin	4s. 6d.	2s. 6d.
Conon	2s. 0d.	1s. 4d.	Lhanbryde	4s. 10d.	3s. 5d.
Muir of Ord	1s. 7d.	1s. 1d.	Fochabers	5s. 4d.	3s. 6d.
Beauly	1s. 3d.	0s. 10d.	Orton Junc.	5s. 8d.	3s. 8d.
Lentran	0s. 9d.	0s. 6d.	Mulben	5s. 10d.	3s. 10d.
Bunchrew	0s. 5d.	0s. 3d.	Keith	6s. 0d.	4s. 0d.
Culloden	0s. 6d.	0s. 4d.	Portsoy	7s. 6d.	5s. 0d.
Dalcross	0s. 8d.	0s. 7d.	Banff	7s. 6d.	5s. 0d.
Fort-George	1s. 2d.	0s. 10d.	Huntly	7s. 6d.	5s. 0d.
Nairn	2s. 0d.	1s. 3d.	Inveramsay	9s. 2d.	6s. 1d.
Brodie	2s. 8d.	1s. 10d.	Inverury	9s. 8d.	6s. 5d.
Forres	3s. 0d.	2s. 0d.	Kintore	9s. 11d.	6s. 7d.
Kinloss	3s. 6d.	2s. 4d.	Aberdeen	11s. 3d.	7s. 6d.
Alves	3s. 10d.	2s. 5d.			

Trains for Inverness leave Aberdeen at 8 A.M. and 4·50 P.M.; Keith at 7·0 A.M., 11 A.M., 4·5 P.M., and 7·40 P.M.

Excursion Tickets for the above may be had at the Booking-Office, Inverness Station, on the Monday previous, up to 8 P.M.

Ask for Excursion Tickets.

Excursion Tickets must be taken out at least Fifteen Minutes before the advertised Time of Starting the Trains, after which Tickets at the Ordinary Fare only will be issued.

For Return Trains at Intermediate Stations, Conditions under which Tickets are issued, and other particulars, see the respective Companies' Monthly Time Bills.

By order.

AND. DOUGALL, *General Manager.*

Railway Office, Inverness, 9th July 1862.

An experienced station master, Mr Miller from Mulben, was appointed to the post at Invergordon. One problem he had soon to deal with was a severe gale which blew down the engine shed on 22nd June.

An Inverness bound train runs across the embankment just after the swing bridge at Clachnaharry. The locomotive is a Big Ben; the number is indistinct but the long name suggests that it is Ben a 'Chaoruinn. The train of 6-wheeled stock seems well filled. *(John Roake collection)*

It is hard to know if the promoters of the original line to Invergordon had any idea how the line would develop. Many improvements were made to the line in later years to handle heavier and more frequent trains. This up goods train on the double track approaching Clachnaharry in LMS days illustrates the line at its peak, with a heavy load of open and covered wagons.

(HRS collection)

An early view of Tain, said to be dated 1864. The locomotive in the siding on the left was not a Highland one, so must have belonged to a contractor. The station building and the water tower have been completed but there is no sign of the goods shed which in September 1864 was said to be under construction. *(HRS collection)*

Between Tain and Bonar Bridge, the railway runs close to the south shore of Dornoch Firth. In this view taken in 2009 from the B9172, which goes over the hills from Alness to Bonar Bridge, the line can be seen cutting a relatively straight path across the fields and then over an embankment in one of the bays on the Firth. *(Keith Fenwick)*

ON TO BONAR BRIDGE

Moves to extend the line northwards were made in early 1862. The next natural place to aim for was Bonar Bridge, the point where the Dornoch Firth narrowed enough to be bridged. From here, the next stage could either go inland via Lairg and then return to the coast or keep to the coast and run eastwards on the north bank of the Firth to Dornoch.

The route from Invergordon was relatively easy; it crossed the flat part of Easter Ross north of Invergordon and then ran close to the edge of the Firth from Tain to the terminus which was actually at Ardgay on the south bank opposite the village of Bonar Bridge.

At the Board meeting on 18th March 1862, the chairman reported that he had attended a meeting in Tain of parties interested in promoting an extension northwards to Bonar Bridge, a distance of 27 miles. The Duke of Sutherland had contributed £30,000 to a subscription list of £50,000. The Board agreed that when a further £20,000 had been subscribed, they would be happy to promote the extension. That goal was reached in October 1862 so it was decided to promote a Bill for the line, with an estimated cost of £5,500 per mile. It seems to have had a relatively easy passage through Parliament, gaining Royal Assent on 11th May 1863 as the Inverness & Aberdeen Junction Railway (Bonar Bridge Extension) Act. This authorised additional capital of £160,000 plus £53,300 borrowing powers under the usual conditions. The shares could be offered as Preference Shares with 3% dividend on the opening of the line then increasing at ½% per year until it was equal to the dividend on ordinary shares; after that the same dividend as on the existing ordinary shares would be paid. By issuing separate shares for this extension, the company avoided diluting returns for existing shareholders but did not need to set up a separate company.

Work commenced during 1863 so that by October the shareholders were informed that it was hoped to open to Tain by Spring of the following year and to Bonar Bridge in June. These predictions were not too far out, even though the initial terminus was altered to Meikle Ferry, 2½ miles beyond Tain. The line was inspected on 31st May and opened on 1st June 1864 with four trains each way. There were stations at Delny, Parkhill, Nigg, Fearn and Tain, although most were still in an unfinished state. Parkhill, Fearn and Tain were described as commodious and handsome buildings. There were passing places at Invergordon, Parkhill and Tain and sidings at Delny, Nigg, Fearn and Meikle Fery. A turntable was provided at Meikle Ferry but engines and tenders had to be uncoupled to use it; this was likely to have been the one installed at Invergordon when the line was extended there. At Meikle Ferry, a tongue of land juts out to form a convenient place for a ferry across the Dornoch Firth and it was expected that the station here would be a permanent feature. This turned out to be an error and it closed in 1869.

The Inspector had commented on the condition of the track. In September, it was reported that the metal chairs were too light and the Company had incurred the expense of replacing them. Three on each rail, which were 6 yards long, were being replaced by heavier ones. At the same time, the "extensive and substantial goods depot" being erected at Tain was almost complete.

Work on the remaining section to Bonar Bridge was complete for Colonel Rich to inspect it in late September and pass it for opening on 1st October. The line was 11 miles 4 chains with stations at Edderton, Mid Fearn and Ardgay. The report in the *Banffshire Journal* says that Rich minutely inspected the bridges along the line and the points and signals at each station. He had "seldom inspected a line where the work was so satisfactory. .... At Invergordon, there is a large roofed-in station. At Delny, as at every other station, very substantial houses were built. The station-houses are generally built so as to embrace offices at one end, waiting rooms and covered promenade or verandah in the centre, and a dwelling house for the station agent at the other end. Behind the station, but within the railway ground, the company are also building cottages for the pointsmen and porters. These are plain houses divided in the centre, with a ground floor and attics, and a separate entrance door to each set of apartments."

Although it was always intended that it would form part of a longer route to the far north, the line to Bonar Bridge was built to meet the demands of the traffic of that part of the country. Substantial station houses were erected but passing places were few. Trains stopped at all stations.

Many of the stations were only completed after opening, so for the first few months make-shift facilities were provided for passengers and goods traffic was restricted. Deciding where to establish stations was not always easy in open country areas. To handle the agricultural traffic, it was useful to have facilities every few miles and this pattern can be seen in the placement of the original stations.

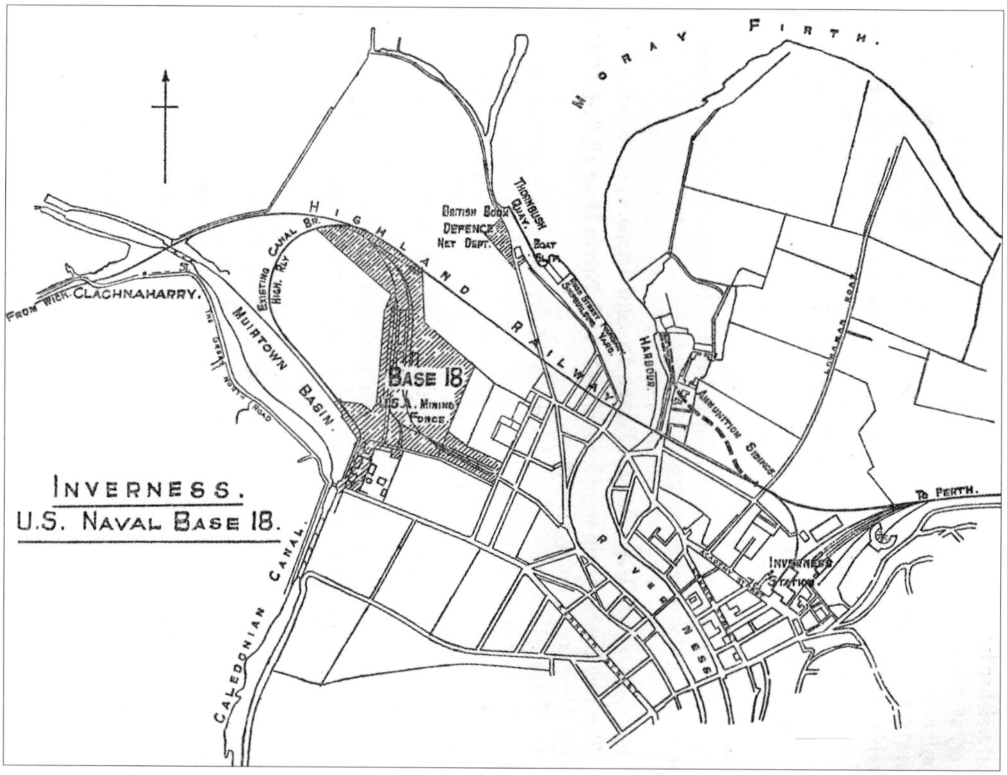

This map of Inverness taken from Edwin Pratt's "British Railways and the Great War" shows not only the extensive development near the Muirtown basin of the Caledonian Canal, but also the general layout at Inverness as far as Clachnaharry.

Part of the Far North Line

After the line was completed through to Wick and Thurso in 1874, the southern section gradually developed as part of the through route. Station facilities were expanded to meet gradually increasing traffic in the latter part of the nineteenth century. Sidings were added for ballast pits, etc. Dingwall underwent considerable expansion, becoming the junction for the Skye line in 1870. Huge changes took place at Invergordon during the First World War and several more sidings were added in the 1970s to deal with the north sea oil traffic and other industrial development.

Passing places were added at most of the stations, initially where needed to handle the gradually increasing train service; after the regulations changed in 1889 the line was completely resignalled with interlocked points and signals and tablet working and several new loops were put in. Most crossing points were provided with two signal boxes with the single line token instruments placed in the booking office. McKenzie & Holland were the contractors for the section south of Invergordon; Dutton resignalled Invergordon and northwards. The Great North of Scotland Railway's design of automatic tablet exchanging apparatus was installed in the 1890s to enable trains to travel safely at speed through crossing stations.

Only one branch, from Muir of Ord to Fortrose, was built, although there were proposals for others, for instance to serve Portmahomack, and construction of the line along the north side of the Black Isle from Conon to Cromarty was well under way in 1914 before the War put a stop to all work; the track which had been laid was lifted and sent to France for the war effort.

That same War put a great strain on the main line as it served the Home Fleet which was based at Scapa Flow for much of the time. More ships were based at Invergordon which was also the main distribution point for mines for the Fleet. Coal and provisions came by sea from Grangemouth and Aberdeen respectively but personnel all went by rail to Thurso. Daily naval specials were operated for much of the War from both Glasgow and London.

By the time the line passed to LMS hands in 1923, its prosperous days were coming to an end. The rise of road transport and the general economic depression of the late 1920s and 1930s resulted in a drop in traffic. By the 1930s, there was an hourly bus service from Inverness to Tain and twice that frequency to Dingwall. With cheaper fares and services often closer to the door, it is no surprise that the buses prospered. Economies were made as a result, mainly by the employment of fewer staff but no attempt was made to improve the train service apart from a late Saturday evening train from Inverness to cater for cinema and theatre goers. That train was so popular that it was difficult to collect all the tickets so some people travelled without buying one.

The Second World War saw another huge increase in traffic. The whole area north of Inverness was restricted. Scapa Flow was once again an important base but there were also several airfields along the flat coastal area right up to the north of Caithness. A limited passenger service was maintained and the Strathpeffer branch reduced to a Saturday only service; that ceased completely in 1946.

Decline set in again once rationing had eased in the 1950s. Service reductions caused by

An early morning scene of much activity in high summer. The overnight train has arrived from the south, this one consisting of mainly East Coast stock, and passengers are crossing to the connection for the Far North line which is waiting in the adjacent platform. Until recent times, it was normal for the morning arrivals from the south to run past the station on the Rose Street curve then back in to a north platform. Conversely trains from the north normally terminated in one of the south platforms to provide easy connection. *(HRS collection)*

the coal shortage of 1951 were not restored and the Black Isle branch lost its passenger service that year. There was talk of closing several stations in the mid-1950s but by 1958 the losses on the line were such that closure of Edderton and all the intermediate stations between Inverness and Tain, except Fearn and Dingwall, was proposed, along with the withdrawal of the local trains to Tain. All that would be left were three trains north to Helmsdale or Wick and Thurso. This aroused considerable local opposition, but to little avail as the closures were implemented on 13th June 1960. A detailed account of the traffic handled at these stations and the closure process can be found in *Lost Stations on the Far North Line.*

These reductions were offered as an alternative to complete closure of the line but the Beeching Report in 1963 proposed just that, along with the Kyle line. A concerted and forceful local campaign and the prospect of several MPs losing their seats at the forthcoming election led to the retention of the lines. A further threat to the Kyle line came with the construction in 1969/70 of the road along the south side of Loch Carron. Built as a single track, the planners in far away places thought that the line could then be closed so that a double track road could take its place. It was only the growth of the north sea oil industry which caused this decision to be reversed.

The closures of 1960, together with the change from steam to diesel traction which was completed in 1961, did allow the through train service to be speeded up and further improvements came in 1964 after the total closure was rejected. Then came the development of the North Sea oil industry, with several plants established in the Invergordon area, and other industrial development such as the Invergordon aluminium smelter, designed to arrest the decline in population in the area. This brought more freight traffic to the line, until improvements in the road network in the 1980s, including the construction of the A9 across the Black Isle, resulted in goods traffic by rail ceasing entirely north of Inverness. On the passenger side, residential development led to the reopening of Alness and Muir of Ord Stations and, eventually, Beauly. There is the prospect of a new station at Conon in the north side of the river.

Parcels traffic, which had held up well during the 1960s due to the lack of any other operator and the popularity of mail order delivery, dropped away during the 1970s. Firstly, local delivery was concentrated at a number of railheads, then rail was not involved at all. Newspaper and mail traffic continued into the early 1980s before it too was lost.

A series of measures has reduced operating costs over the years. Mechanical signalling was becoming expensive to staff and maintain and was replaced by Radio Tokenless Block in the mid 1980s. All signalling was now controlled from Inverness and the remaining few staff at each station were withdrawn. Invergordon and Tain retained staff for ticket sales and enquiries for a few more years, but by the early 1990s, only Dingwall had staff, and then for only part of the day.

Diesel multiple units replaced locomotive hauled trains in the late 1980s. Thus by the early 1990s, the line was operated by a few train crews and a signalman at Inverness, plus one at Clachnaharry when the canal is open. Track maintenance was mechanised and the number of track workers reduced. One team, based at Dingwall, covers the line from Inverness to Bonar Bridge and beyond. If anything goes wrong, help takes a long time to come.

A major threat to the continued existence of the line north of Inverness came when the Ness viaduct collapsed on 7th February 1989 after heavy rains undermined its piers. The destruction was fortunately detected in time to stop any trains approaching it. Several diesel units and locomotives were stranded north of the break, so it was possible to organise a service from Dingwall with connecting buses between there and Inverness. With rebuilding expected to take several months, maintenance facilities were required and these were set up in the former goods yard at Muir of Ord. Heavy maintenance could not be undertaken there so it was necessary to transfer several vehicles by road to and from the isolated north lines. Given the importance of the lines to the local community, funds were quickly made available to rebuild the bridge and to construct it to handle all traffic. The new structure was formally reopened on 9th May 1990 in time for the summer timetable which started on 14th May. Its concrete form, supported by two piers, is in stark contrast to the original, but it is capable of handling the heaviest passenger and freight trains.

The last few years have been a period of some growth. The Friends of the Far North Line have focussed attention of the use of the line and its importance to the local economy. Inverness has expanded dramatically and now suffers from severe rush hour congestion. Additional services have been introduced on the southern end of the Far North line, starting with trains from Dingwall and then from Tain. The line now enjoys its best service ever with four trains each way to Wick and four to Kyle plus shorter workings to Invergordon, Tain and Ardgay to provide a better spread of services on the busier section. Unlike many bus services, the trains continue running late into the evening. A passenger leaving Edinburgh or Glasgow at 17.40 can reach Tain at 22.15. An even later service is provided on Friday and Saturday nights, not reaching Tain until 00.35. A Sunday service is provided throughout the year.

The 10.30am to Kyle ready to depart in June 1957. This part of the station was added when the line to Dingwall was opened; the connection avoiding the station can be seen in the foreground. The train, behind Black 5 No.44719, includes as the second vehicle the ex-Highland Railway Travelling Post Office which was left at Dingwall to be taken north to Helmsdale on the 10.50am to Wick. Black Fives were the main motive power from the late 1930s until 1960/61 when diesels took over.

(Sandy Edwards/GNSRA)

The approach to the Ness Viaduct from the station in May 1965. The track immediately to the right of the running line led down to the harbour, with sidings further to the right. Two sidings remain here and are occasionally used for storage or shunting. *(J L Stevenson)*

Inverness to Dingwall

The line north from Inverness was single throughout. When opened, trains could only pass at Beauly but over the years loops were added at Lentran, Clunes, Muir of Ord and Conon as well as at Bruichnain (2 miles 58 chains from Inverness) which was opened in 1902. Further growth led to the installation of double track from Clachnaharry, just beyond where the line passes under the old A9, to Clunes in 1913. This was reduced to single track in the 1960s when a loop was put in again at Lentran.

The layout of Inverness station did not easily lend itself to serving the north. The line from Nairn ran on a long curve towards the terminus facing Academy Street. Just before, a line branched away towards the harbour. For the Ross-shire Railway, new terminal platforms were built with their buffer stops adjacent to the existing ones but curving in the opposite direction towards the bridge over the Ness just south of the harbour branch; ships could no longer berth on the shallower section upriver from the bridge.

On the approach to the bridge, a ticket platform, known as Innes Street, was opened on 1st May 1868, although the Board had resolved as early as 1863 to erect it. Up trains stopped there so that tickets did not have to be collected at Inverness station. It remained in use at least until 1898 but its subsequent history is unclear. It may have disappeared during the rebuilding work at that time but there is a further decision recorded in 1909 to provide a Ticket Platform there and this was in situ in 1917. Clachnaharry was also used to collect tickets when it was open. There was a signal box at the south end of the viaduct known as Ness Viaduct. This was closed in 1936 when its token instruments were moved to Rose Street, the box at the end of the north line platforms in Inverness station.

To cross the river, a fine four-arch stone bridge was constructed to the design of Joseph Mitchell. This withstood many floods until 7th February 1989 when, as already noted, it was washed away. The present concrete bridge was then built speedily and was ready for the 1990 summer timetable.

The line then continues along the flat area close to the shore. On 9th April 1877 a branch was opened to serve the Muirtown basin of the Caledonian Canal. This carried only freight traffic which continued until the 1960s; it was put out of use on 31st December 1969. During the First World War, this branch was taken over to serve US Naval Base 18 which was constructed between the main line and the Muirtown Basin, as shown on page 18. This was used for the assembly of mines, the parts for which were brought through the Caledonian Canal. Traffic started arriving in April 1918.

The line now reached the Caledonian Canal at Clachnaharry. This required a swing bridge as, unlike many other canals, the Caledonian is designed for sea going ships and does not have any overbridges. The bridge was renewed in 1909 to allow heavier engines to cross it. Operating and maintaining this bridge is expensive. A signalman has to be on duty throughout the period the canal is open to traffic and the operating mechanism must ensure that the rails are properly aligned and the bridge locked in position before a train can cross. Detailed instructions were issued for the operation of the bridge. The bridge was electrically interlocked with the tablet for the Ness Viaduct to Clachnaharry section for which the normal allowance was 4 minutes,

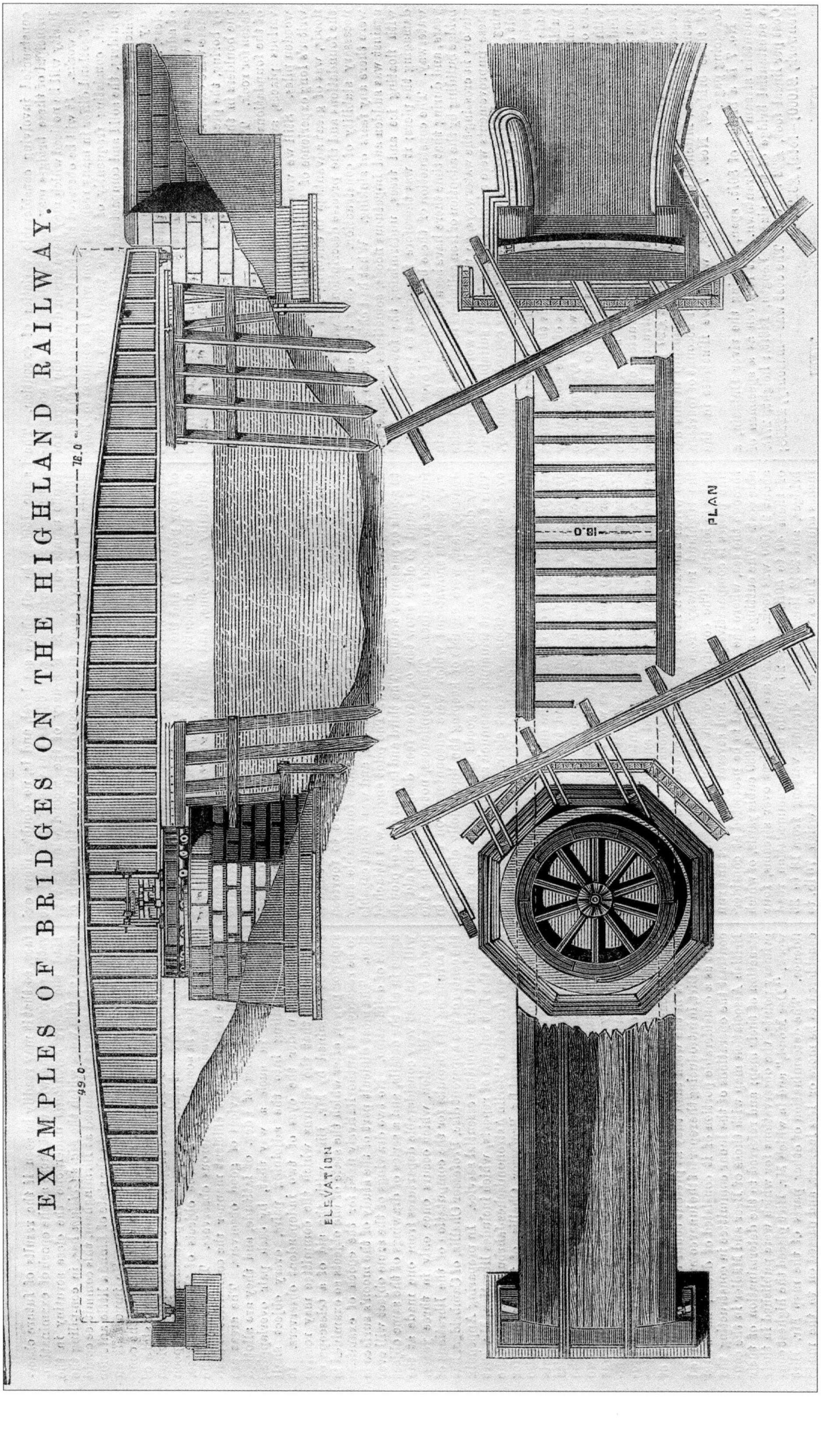

Details of the bridge at Clachnaharry from The Engineer *13th September 1867.*

(Left) Clachmaharry swing bridge looking towards Dingwall. The interlocking which ensures that the bridge is in position for rail traffic is prominent in the foreground.
(Keith Fenwick)

(Below) Speedy operation of the swing bridge at Clachnaharry is essential to avoid delays to either rail or canal traffic but for many years it was manually operated and two people were needed.
(HRS collection)

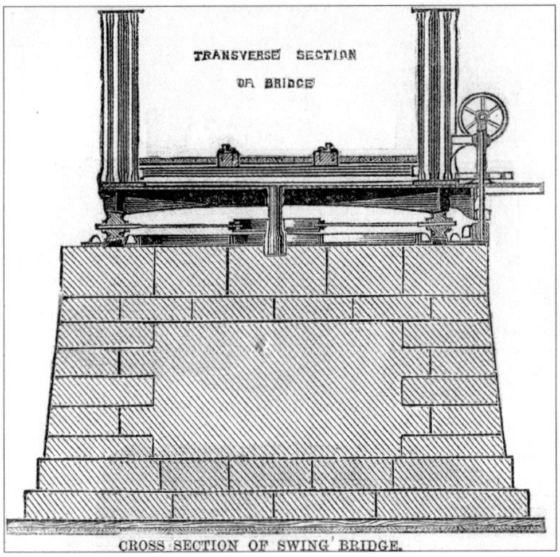

with an allowance for releasing and restoring the tablets, every train prevented canal use for 6 or 7 minutes. Mail and express passenger trains were given priority over canal traffic but local passenger and goods trains could be delayed. The stationmaster at Bunchrew and the signalman at Ness Viaduct had to warn the Clachnaharry signalman of approaching trains.

Immediately beyond the canal bridge was Clachnaharry station (1m 61c), opened on 1st April 1868 and closed on 1st April 1913. No sidings were ever provided here. The line from here to Clunes was doubled in June 1913 in time for the summer traffic but to avoid rebuilding the narrow road bridge at the west end of the station this commenced on the other side of that bridge. That was too far away from the signal box for the points to be operated, so they were placed on the Inverness side of the bridge and interlaced track installed through the bridge. This was replaced in early LMS days with remotely operated points beyond the bridge.

The line is now clear of the built-up area and runs along the shore next to the road. The first intermediate station at the line's opening was at Bunchrew (3m 34c), adjacent to the level crossing. It appears that Bunchrew did not initially handle goods traffic as the Board later agreed to a request from farmers and others in the district for a siding there. The station building is now a private house but the level crossing, with its limited line of sight along the railway, remains. Bunchrew was closed to passengers on 13th June 1960, as were all the

Bunchrew looking towards Inverness in September 1956. The double track was still in place and passengers had the benefit of three trains to Inverness and two in the return direction. The level crossing in the foreground now has warning lights and no barrier and is still a hazard. *(J L Stevenson)*

other stations between Inverness and Dingwall. Goods services continued until 1964. Near the station, there was a source of ballast for the railway. A new siding was provided here in 1901 and another further on in 1923. In 1918, a siding for timber traffic was inspected; this was at the west end of the station and connected to the down line, but worked from the signal box.

Lentran (5m 45c) is the next station. This had a wooden building which deteriorated after the station closed and was eventually demolished a few years ago, to be replaced by housing.

Lentran looking south in September 1956. The station was well maintained with trimmed hedges. The pillared verandah of the rather ramshackle wooden building is behind the footbridge. *(J L Stevenson)*

Clunes looking towards Beauly in September 1956. The small wooden station building was on the left behind the footbridge and beyond that were a couple of sidings. The double track ended at the signal box in the distance. *(J L Stevenson)*

Goods traffic ceased in 1964, but the sidings were retained for a tar depot which served the whole of the north of Scotland. This continued into the 1970s. When this section of the line was singled, a passing place was once again provided here but it was removed in the 1980s.

Clunes (7m 29c) served Kirkhill, which was some distance away, and was not opened with the line. A request for a station here was noted in the Minutes of 11th August 1862 but it was not until 23rd April 1863 that this was agreed to as a trial. A small siding was to be provided. The station opened on 1st October 1863. The loop was added here in 1904, along with the down platform. Traffic fell off when road services started but it was still popular with local school children until closure.

Back on the single track, the line headed for Beauly but first had to cross the river. The original wooden bridge here was replaced by a steel structure as described on page 10. Beauly (9m 67c) had a substantial building on the up platform which included a private waiting room for Lord Lovat. The station also served the local sawmill on the north side of the A9 road bridge; this in turn had a narrow gauge railway running south west, initially alongside the A9, from the station to bring timber down from the hills. A siding was laid in at the south end of the station during the Second World War for the Ministry of Supply. The station was sited some distance from the centre of the town, so it too closed in 1960 but, after considerable campaigning, was reopened on 15th April 2002. As the station building is now in private use and track had been moved, a new platform had to be built on the west side of the line. To keep costs to a minimum, this was so short that trains have to stop with the centre door at the platform and only one door is opened.

The line runs behind the town of Beauly and on to Muir of Ord (12m 61c) where the station was beside the A9 road overbridge. When the line was inspected, this station was named as Tarradale and this appeared in the first timetable published in the *Inverness Courier*. However, by the middle of the following month it was shown as Muir of Ord. Given the haste with

A handsome building was erected at Beauly which included a personal waiting room for Lord Lovat. This photograph taken in 1956 looks towards Inverness, with the goods yard on the left. The building is now a private house and trains use a short new platform on the right. *(J L Stevenson)*

The A9 road overbridge provided an ideal view of Muir of Ord. The down platform is on the right. Fortrose trains arrived at the outer edge of the island platform on the left. The grain silos were constructed on the spare ground in the distance on the left. Trains can still cross here; northbound trains run on the left track and southbound ones on the right to simplify access to the sidings.
(Ian Scrimgeour/Neil Sinclair colln)

which the line was opened after the Board of Trade inspection, perhaps the Company had not decided on the name to be used.

The OS map surveyed in 1872 shows that all parts of the station were south of the A9 bridge and included one main platform, several sidings and cattle pens. There was considerable traffic to the local cattle mart, with a special platform somewhere to the south of the station in early years. The opening of the Black Isle branch to Fortrose on 1st February 1894 led to the extension of the down platform under the road bridge and construction of a bay platform at the north end plus an island platform, which also extended under the road bridge, on the up side. Further signalling alterations were made in 1925, when the single line token instruments were moved from the booking office to the respective boxes and double line signalling introduced between the two boxes.

The Black Isle branch, which curved away to the east through what is now a housing estate, lost its passenger service on 1st October 1951 and was closed completely on 13th June 1960. In the 1960s, a grain silo was built at the station and this kept the station busy for many years but its use ceased in the 1980s. The north sea oil boom in the 1970s led to demands for better transport in the area, so the station was reopened for passengers on 4th October 1976 using the original platforms which had survived. When the Ness Viaduct was washed away in 1989, a maintenance depot was established on spare ground at the south of the station so that trains could continue operating in the far north, although services started from Dingwall. In May 1999, the station building, which dated from the reconstruction in the 1890s and was untypically for the Highland in rendered brick, was demolished and replaced by a bus-stop shelter.

Conon (15m 78c) served the small village of that name and also Maryburgh, on the other side of the river. For many years the station consisted of a single platform on the east, or village,

Muir of Ord in May 1989 when the Ness Viaduct was being rebuilt and the maintenance depot in the distance was in operation. Class 156 units worked most of the services then, but loco hauled stock and class 37s were still available for the peak summer traffic. *(Keith Fenwick)*

side of the line with sidings beyond. It was rebuilt with a passing place in the early years of the 20th century and would have been a junction if construction of the Cromarty & Dingwall Light Railway had been completed. This was in progress when the First World War broke out and it was later abandoned. The River Conon is crossed on a fine five arch stone bridge which was regarded as an engineering achievement at the time. It has five arches with 73 feet spans on a skew of 45° to the river. The north abutment is 304 feet downstream from the south one. A series of right-angled stone ribs spans from pier to pier. The village of Maryburgh has seen considerable growth in recent years and there has been strong support for a station.

Conon in its original state with a single platform and rather overgrown track. The rebuilt station below shows a new signalbox. The Cromarty line would have run off to the right past the goods shed.
(Above LGRP, below J L Stevenson)

Dingwall (18m 34c) was the initial terminus of the line and is one of the largest towns north of Inverness. This was another station which grew over the years. It is not known what the initial layout was, as by the time of the first Ordnance Survey in 1873, the line to Skye had been opened. The station then consisted of two main through platforms plus a third on the other side of the up platform, together with sidings and engine shed on the west side at the south end. The present substantial stone building dates from 1886 and is similar in style to a number of contemporary Highland station reconstructions. The large down platform is covered by a glazed awning. On the up side, several sidings were added at a later date for exchange of traffic in the area which is now covered in trees. The engine shed housed locos for the Strathpeffer line and some of the Kyle services as well as a local shunter. With dieselisation and the drop in traffic, the local pilot was withdrawn at the end of 1961 and the shed closed. Most of the goods yard and the site of the engine shed were sold for housing development in the 1990s. The bay platform was out of use by the late 1960s and the track removed. The area has just been left since then, so the trees have taken over.

Immediately north of Dingwall, the line crosses the Dingwall Canal. The Act required a swing bridge here unless the Town Council, who owned the Canal, agreed to a fixed bridge. The Canal had actually become a burden on the Council, so when £500 and construction of a new wharf on the seaward side of the bridge was offered by the railway, the Council readily agreed.

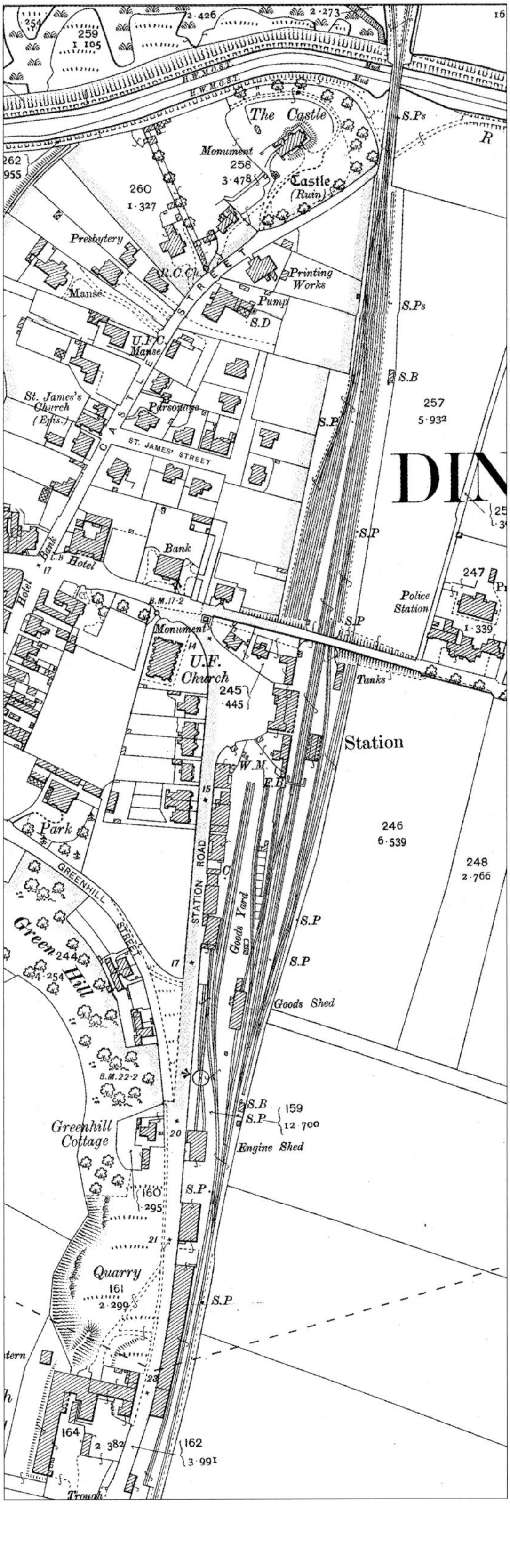

Dingwall on the 25 inch OS map published in 1906. (Reproduced by permission of the Trustees of the National Library of Scotland)

Dingwall from the footbridge, looking north, in August 1969. The barrow on the platform is full of parcels and the Post Office mail van is waiting on the platform. Although there is still track on the outer side of the island platform on the right, it is no longer in use. Beyond the main building the separate wooden building, now the Mallard pub, served refreshments to servicemen during the Second World War. *(Keith Fenwick)*

Looking the other way from the same footbridge, the morning Wick and Thurso train arrives at Dingwall in August 1969. Although the loco shed, which was beyond the goods shed, had been demolished, other facilities remained. Cattle traffic had ceased by then so the wagons in the overgrown siding would have been waiting disposal. The sidings on the left were also out of use; these had been extended during the Second World War and then used for wagon storage during the early 1960s. *(Keith Fenwick)*

Dingwall to Invergordon

Only enough land for a single track was purchased for the section to Invergordon and thus it has remained. Initially there was a passing place at Novar with another added at Alness and then, during the First World War, at Foulis.

From Dingwall, the line headed in a north-easterly direction along the north side of the Cromarty Firth. The first station was the isolated one at Fowlis (22m 51c), renamed Foulis in 1916 and pronounced 'fowls'. This served the house of the same name, the home of the Munro family of whom Sir Hector was a director of the Highland Railway. One of the Castle class locomotives was named *Foulis Castle*. There was a level crossing over a minor road here with a single platform just before it. Originally there was a siding next to the platform but this was moved to the other side of the crossing in 1878 and cattle pens and a loading bank added to handle the agricultural traffic of the district. A small building on the platform provided the station facilities while there was a separate station master's house; this remains but much modernised. To allow for increased war time traffic, a passing place was built just to the south of the station in 1916 which continued in use until 1949. The station closed completely on 13th June 1960.

Evanton (24m 58c) was just north of the village of the same name and quite close to Novar House, by which name the station was known until 1937. Perhaps it had been located north of the village to serve the house, but this meant that when bus services started along the A9 they were more convenient. The building here was a long, single storey one in stone with

Foulis had a small station master's house and a separate wooden building for the station users. The house remains, although it has a new, higher, roof. The photographer was standing on the level crossing; the loop was out of sight to the left towards Dingwall. (C L Kerr)

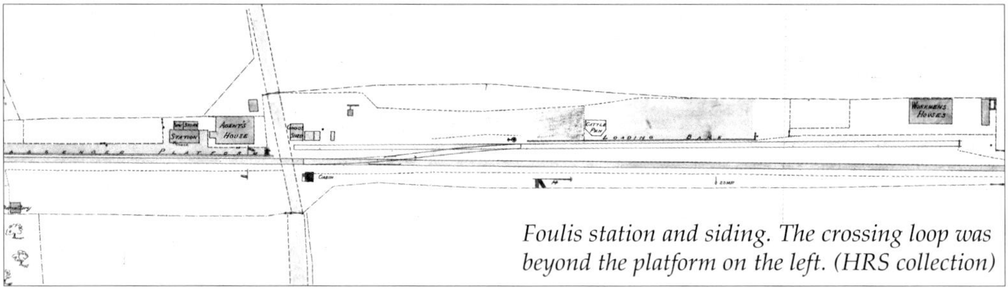

Foulis station and siding. The crossing loop was beyond the platform on the left. (HRS collection)

Evanton looking south from the footbridge in 1956. The main station building is on the right with the road, at that time the A9, curving away towards the village. The sidings were behind the photographer. (J L Stevenson)

The stone bridge at Alness - two arches of 60 foot span. (HRS/Roberts collection)

Alness looking south in 1956 with the station building on the right and the goods yard beyond. The siding behind the platform on the left led to Dalmore Distillery. *(J L Stevenson)*

an awning supported by iron pillars along the platform side. Passenger services ceased on 13th June 1960 and goods on 2nd November 1964. The building fell into disrepair and was eventually demolished. The station was the scene of an accident in 1872. An up goods train was waiting to cross the down mail train when the station master allowed it to draw forward to pick up some sacks of potatoes which had been stacked by the line. It failed to return before the mail arrived and in the ensuing collision, eight passengers were injured.

The story of the next few miles is complicated by the changes during the First World War for naval traffic and later for industrial development. Dealing with the main stations, the first is Alness (28m 25c), a busy station situated conveniently for the town. It had a large Italianate style building which combined station facilities and station master's house. Similar buildings were constructed at several of the Ross-shire stations as well as on the line to Keith. A siding to the adjacent Dalmore Distillery was opened in 1878. Alness was one of the more contentious passenger closures when it lost its service on 13th June 1960 but with industrial development in the area, service was restored on 7th May 1973. Today it is often busier than Invergordon as the town has grown considerably. Goods services ceased in June 1983, although by that time there would have been very little traffic.

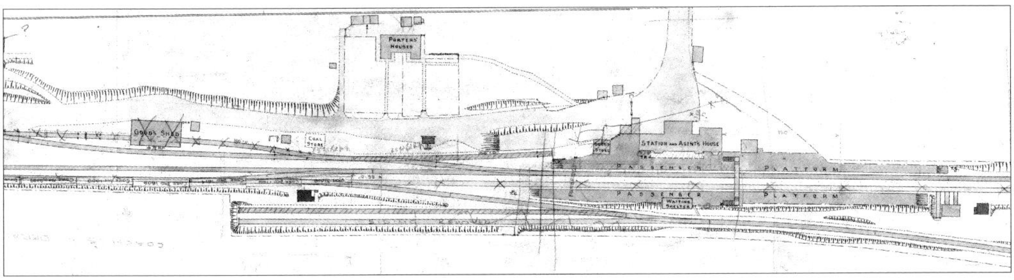

Details of the layout at Alness are shown on this plan which has been marked up to show track which had to be removed after closure of the station. The line at the bottom right led to Dalmore distillery.

Invergordon from the 1906 25 inch OS map, showing part of the harbour branch before the developments of World War 1.
(Reproduced by permission of the Trustees of the National Library of Scotland)

Invergordon station looking north in 1973, when mail traffic was still handled. The sidings were to the right of the building, which originally had an overall roof. *(Norris Forrest/GNSRA)*

The line now runs almost due east to Invergordon (31m 12c). The station is situated towards the south end of the burgh. The station building is quite unlike any other on the line, actually two single storey structures separated by an arched entrance from the road. Originally there was a roof over the tracks and the first edition OS map suggests that, although there was a loop, only one platform was provided. No photographs in this condition are known. An extensive goods yard was sited at the south end, on the seaward side.

Invergordon was a significant port before the railway came, so it was natural that a siding was built to serve the harbour. This left the main line just before the station and ran along the shore, past the ferry slip and the harbour to terminate at the Bone Mill.

It was the First World War which brought major changes in this area. Invergordon was established as a naval dockyard for the repair of ships, which employed about 4,000 workers. An oil fuel depot for those modern warships which were oil fired was also set up. A new pier was constructed.

A gravel pit was opened up ½ mile south of Alness in May 1916 to provide stone to enable the foreshore at Invergordon to be reclaimed. Up to three special trains ran per day to Invergordon with the traffic until January 1917, the number of trains being limited by the heavy traffic on the line.

In June 1916, an engineering shop was erected at the end of Dalmore Distillery siding; here plates were shaped and bored for the decks of ships which had to be strengthened after the damage experienced in the Battle of Jutland. Delivery of 2,000 tons of plates a month was involved.

New piers were constructed at Invergordon and the branch extended. Huts to accommodate about 7,000 workers were erected; a siding referred to as 'Hutment Siding' was provided for Admiralty traffic in 1916, 100 yards north of the Alness up distant.

After the USA entered the War in 1917, it was decided to erect the Northern Barrage, a huge minefield extending from the Orkneys to the Norwegian Coast using materials supplied

Extensive sidings were laid in at Invergordon for the Aluminium smelter but by April 1991, when this photograph was taken, the site had been closed down. *(Keith Fenwick)*

by the USA which were shipped to Kyle of Lochalsh. Dalmore Distillery was requisitioned and converted into workshops and stores, known as "US Naval Base 17". As the bonded warehouses were to be used, the whisky stored there had to be moved to the distillery at Edderton. The existing siding from Alness did not terminate in a suitable place to serve these workshops, so Belleport Siding was constructed from the main line 1½ miles north of Alness with points facing up trains. This carried a passenger service for workers.

Ships arrived at Kyle about once every fortnight; three or four trains, limited to 11 wagons each, were worked daily for about a week to Dalmore. Once the mines were assembled they were taken to Invergordon by an extra set of rails laid for about 4 miles along one side of the road, using rails recovered from the recently closed Buckie branch. A pier was under construction at Dalmore for this traffic, but it was not completed until after the Armistice; it was useful in 1921 when the Barrage was being dismantled.

As well as extra trains to these facilities, traffic had to be shunted when it arrived. An intriguing entry in the Weekly Circulars from 1915 read :

PUG ENGINE DINGWALL TO INVERGORDON

> Every weekday until further notice, a pug engine leaves Dingwall for Invergordon at 7.0a.m. and returns at 4.0p.m. Dingwall to attach Third Class Carriages for Railway Servants from Alness to Invergordon.

In 1918, in response to the request from the Highland Railway for locomotives from other companies, the Great Western Railway lent a steam railmotor and this was used on this service. It was not very reliable. Some of the additional traffic continued for a few years after the War as the facilities served were gradually run down.

Life at Invergordon gradually returned to normal. The Second World War saw increased traffic at the town, but nothing on the scale of a quarter of a century earlier and no extra facilities were needed there.

The 1960s and 1970s saw considerable development in the Invergordon area. A new siding for the Distillery was opened north of the station in 1965 and then came the North Sea oil boom. Invergordon and Nigg Bay were developed as major construction sites. Initially, most of the materials were brought in by rail and goods traffic to the area surged. The harbour branch was used and a new site developed for MK Shand to the north of the town which required two separate sidings. Another initiative was the Invergordon Aluminium Smelter, again to the north of the town, but this proved a commercial failure and closed during December 1981. Once the A9 between Perth and Invergordon had been improved in the 1980s, rail ceased to be competitive. In any case, the demands of the oil industry shifted from construction to maintenance and less material had to be brought in. Goods traffic at Invergordon ceased on 1st May 1987, the other sidings in the area having closed some years before.

Loading mines at Invergordon harbour during the First World War. Wagons have brought the assembled mines from the facility at Alness for loading into barges. The pier is in the distance.
(Imperial War Museum)

Pre-printed labels were available for passengers luggage to a huge variety of destinations, such as this example for journeys from Aberdeen to Novar. It was printed on yellow gummed paper.

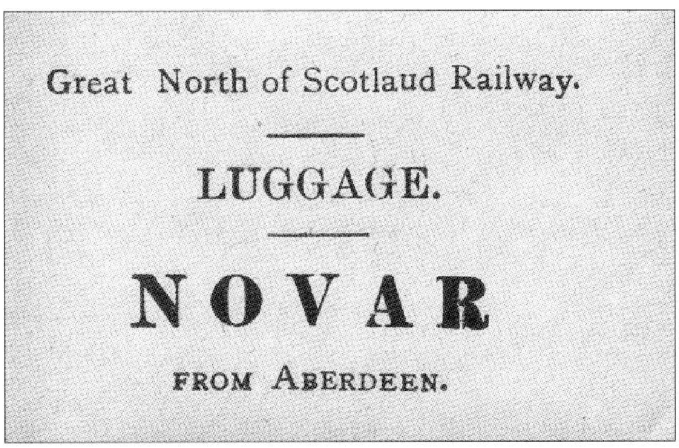

Great North of Scotlaud Railway.

LUGGAGE.

NOVAR

FROM ABERDEEN.

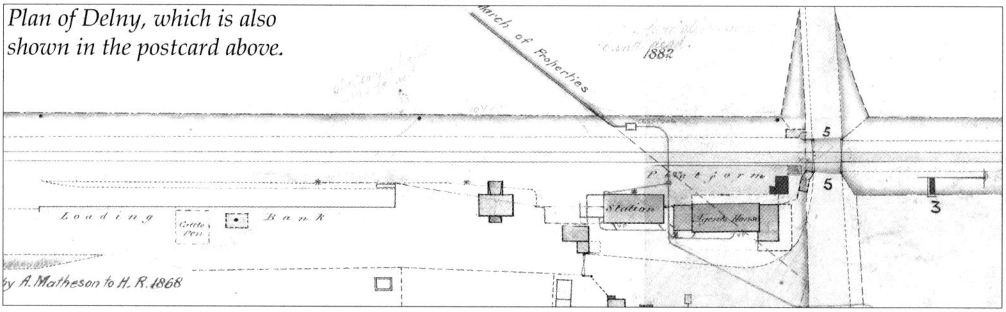

Plan of Delny, which is also shown in the postcard above.

The station building at Kildary was on the south side of the line which headed in a north easterly direction at this point. This view from 1956 looks towards Parkhill bridge, with the sidings on the left behind the photographer. (C J B Sanderson/J L Stevenson collection)

North of Invergordon

The line from Invergordon to Meikle Ferry was inspected on 30th May 1864 and the remainder to Bonar Bridge on 1st October 1864. It was reported that the line was single with passing places at Parkhill and Tain. There was a turntable at Meikle Ferry, which may have been the one in temporary use at Invergordon. It was so short that the loco and tender had to be separated. Passing places were later provided at Fearn and Edderton. All the stations to Bonar Bridge except Fearn and Tain closed to passengers on 13th June 1960.

From Invergordon, the track runs parallel to the shore but about half a mile inland for some miles and therefore not very convenient for the scattered hamlets on the foreshore. The first station, Delny (35m 53c), had a single platform next to a level crossing and a simple stone building for the station offices next to a pair of staff cottages. It served the village of Barbaraville on the shore of Nigg Bay but was named after the nearby Delny House. Freight services survived until 15th June 1964.

The next station (36m 35c) was one of those built to serve the general district and not a particular place. Originally it was called Parkhill, but that conflicted with the station of the same name on the Great North of Scotland Railway's Peterhead line, so the Board decided to change it to Kildary in December 1865 at the request of the GNSR. It had a larger Italianate building similar to that at Alness. A passing loop was provided here and a small goods yard which continued in use until 25th January 1965.

Nigg (38m 79c) was optimistically named as the village of the same name was over 3 miles away. The small hamlet which grew up around it was known as Nigg Station, as was the local Post Office. The building here was of a different style to nearby stations and consisted of

Parkhill bridge, to the north of Kildary station, dated from 1864 and had a 50 foot span.
(HRS/Roberts collection)

The northbound morning mail, on the left, must have been late as on this occasion in the 1950s it crossed the 12.5pm local at Kildary instead of getting to Tain before the local left. No doubt that enabled the enterprising photographer time to nip onto the footbridge to take this shot. The roof of the Highland TPO can just be made out in front of the Gresley-designed Restaurant Car on Wick train; both would come off at Helmsdale. The local is headed by a 'Caley Bennie', as the Caledonian 4-4-0s were referred to by drivers on the Highland. *(John Roake collection)*

The station at Nigg had a similar layout to that at Delny but it boasted a superior station building. Even so, it had been necessary to add an extra wooden building for storage on the platform. This photo was taken in June 1956 and is looking north. *(C J B Sanderson/J L Stevenson collection)*

Fearn on a sunny evening in June 1956. The photo is taken from the road overbridge at the Tain end of the station. (C J B Sanderson/J L Stevenson collection)

station master's house at right angles to the platform and offices in a wing facing the platform. Goods facilities were withdrawn on 26th December 1964.

The line is now well inland with rising ground on the inland side and the prosperous agricultural land of Easter Ross on the seaward side. Fearn (40m 30c) served the village of Hill of Fearn and the area out to Portmahomack. It had a large building similar to Alness and a passing loop was added on the west side, although it is hard today to see any evidence of it. The large goods yard dealt with the agricultural traffic of the district which included

Tain in July 1969 seen from an up afternoon train. Mail is being loaded onto the train. The goods yard was on the other side of the main building. (Keith Fenwick)

Tain from the bridge at the north end of the station in August 1955. The siding on the left held spare carriages. Just to the right of the platforms, a Black Five can be seen shunting in the sidings, while to the right of the signal box is an 'Atcost' pre-cast concrete building, a type installed at a number of stations in the 1950s for storage mainly of animal feedstuffs. *(J L Stevenson)*

considerable quantities of seed potatoes in the autumn. This traffic continued throughout the 1960s so it remained open for goods traffic after the other stations on this section had closed. It was then in a good position to deal with steel for the construction of North Sea oil platforms in Nigg Bay. This continued during the 1970s but ceased during the 1980s.

A change of direction follows, with the course now generally north west as far as Lairg. Tain (44m) is another long-established burgh. As this was also the terminus of local services from Inverness it had quite a large station. The main building, again Italianate in design, was single storey and H-shaped, with a long central section with awning. The station master's accommodation was separate. The early view on page 16 of the station from the town shows that the Dornoch Firth was quite close, but today silting has pushed it further away. The large goods yard was on the town side at the north end of the station. This continued in use until the 1970s, when traffic died off.

Several locomotives were based here in the shed which was on the seaward side of the line just before the station was reached. There was no room for a turntable here, so it was originally installed in the goods yard. A larger turntable was needed in the late 1930s and this was built in the field behind the southbound platform. In the 1950s, the shed housed a couple of Caledonian 4-4-0s but these were withdrawn in 1960 when the Tain local trains finished and the shed was then closed.

For the next few miles the line runs close to the south side of the Dornoch Firth. Glenmorangie Distillery (45m 19c) was served by a private siding which remained in use until June 1970. To avoid the long detour by road to Bonar Bridge, a ferry was established at the narrow point next to where the modern A9 road bridge crosses the Firth. Meikle Ferry (46m 40c) was built to serve this and provided with a substantial building similar to Alness but once the railway reached Golspie, its use must have declined so much that the Board decided to close station on 1st January 1869. Its building remained and became the Meikle Ferry Inn. Today it has been modernised but the railway features remain prominent and it is now known,

The Dornoch Bridge Inn in 2009 was instantly recognisable by its design as the former Meikle Ferry station. This is the view from the approach road. The spit of land which once led to the Ferry and now leads to he Dornoch Bridge is to the right. *(Keith Fenwick)*

more appropriately, as the Dornoch Bridge Inn. The access road is from the roundabout at the end of the bridge.

The first village after Tain was Edderton (48m 29c). The building here shows similarities to Nigg. With a conservatory added, the building is now a private residence. At the north end of the station was a small goods yard, closed on 2nd November 1964, then a siding to Balblair Distillery. During the Second World War, this was used by Norwegian troops and was visited by King Haakon.

Edderton in August 1955 looking towards Bonar Bridge with Balblair Distillery in the background. *(J L Stevenson)*

Another interesting survivor is the small building at Mid Fearn, seen looking south in 1955. *(J L Stevenson)*

A small station was opened at Mid Fearn (54m 78c) to serve Fearn Lodge but it had little other use so was closed to the public on 31st March 1865. The 1920 Appendix shows that it was in use as a request stop when Mid Fearn Lodge was occupied and this may have been the situation since 1865. Use by school children was noted in the 1930s. The platform survived until at least the 1950s and the building still stands but is very dilapidated.

There were three separate sidings on this part of the line. Ardvannie, opened in 1911, was 1½ miles north of Edderton and served a quarry which supplied ballast for the railway. Mid Fearn Timber siding was opened in 1917 and Ardchronie, 2¾ miles south of Bonar Bridge, was opened in 1919 or 1920 for Easter Ross District Committee for road metal; the Committee allowed a local timber merchant, Messrs Fiddes & Co., to load timber here. It is not know how

Bonar Bridge had a typical goods yard, with three sidings; there was a platform on the one on the left, the middle one could be used to unload into carts or lorries and the third one ran into the goods shed. The signal box on the right controlled access to the sidings and the south end points. There was another one at the far end, beyond the road bridge, to control the points at the north end while the single line token instruments were kept in the main building. *(J L Stevenson)*

long any of these lasted but Ardchonie may have remained in use after the others.

The village of Bonar Bridge grew up on the north side of the bridge over the Firth but the station of that name (57m 43c) was about a mile away in the village of Ardgay. To avoid confusion the station was renamed Ardgay on 2nd May 1977. It boasted another building similar to Alness, the last one up the line to do so, as well as a large goods yard which remained available for use until January 1984. It was a convenient station for Dornoch as, although The Mound was nearer, that was several miles further along the line to the north. In the 1950s, it was again used for freight from Dornoch; the cost of road transport from Dornoch to Bonar Bridge was less than the charge by rail the long way round via The Mound and Lairg. The road bridge over the line at the west end of the station was built when the railway was extended to Golspie.

Bonar Bridge looking north in the 1970s, when the northbound platform had been shortened.

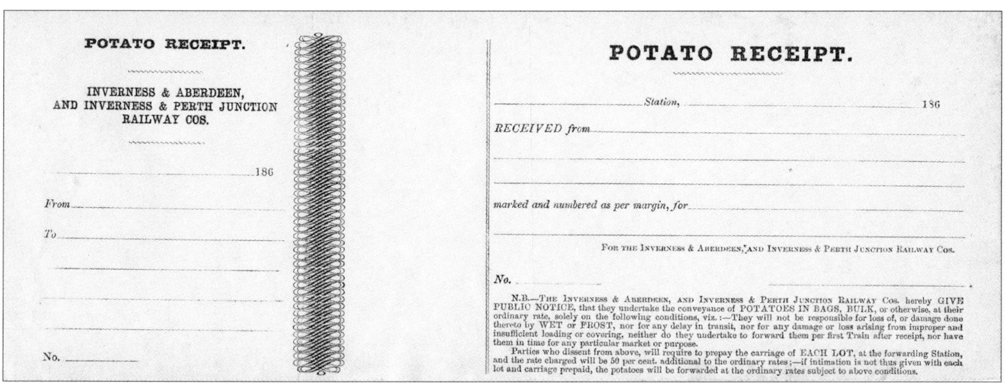

POTATO RECEIPT.

INVERNESS & ABERDEEN,
AND INVERNESS & PERTH JUNCTION
RAILWAY COS.

.... 186

From ....

To ....

No. ....

POTATO RECEIPT.

.... *Station,* 186

RECEIVED from ....

marked and numbered as per margin, for ....

FOR THE INVERNESS & ABERDEEN, AND INVERNESS & PERTH JUNCTION RAILWAY COS.

No. ....

N.B.—THE INVERNESS & ABERDEEN, AND INVERNESS & PERTH JUNCTION RAILWAY COS. hereby GIVE PUBLIC NOTICE, that they undertake the conveyance of POTATOES IN BAGS, BULK, or otherwise, at their ordinary rate, solely on the following conditions, viz.:—They will not be responsible for loss of, or damage done thereto by WET or FROST, nor for any delay in transit, nor for any damage or loss arising from improper and insufficient loading or covering, neither do they undertake to forward them per first Train after receipt, nor have them in time for any particular market or purpose.

Parties who dissent from above, will require to prepay the carriage of EACH LOT, at the forwarding Station, and the rate charged will be 50 per cent. additional to the ordinary rates;—if intimation is not thus given with each lot and carriage prepaid, the potatoes will be forwarded at the ordinary rates subject to above conditions.

Potatoes were always and important traffic on the line south of Tain, even in very early days.

LMS Timetable for July 1938. This illustrates the line at its busiest in pre-war days.

INVERNESS, DINGWALL, INVERGORDON, BONAR BRIDGE, GEORGEMAS, and WICK

Miles.	Down.	Week Days.												
		mrn	P	mrn	mrn	mrn	mrn	B	mrn	mrn	mrn	aft	aft	aft
	746 PERTH (Gen.) dep.	1N20	1N20	1N20	5B5	5 5	6 25	6 25	9 30	1155	11†55	1210	3 55	6 5
	746 AVIEMORE .. "	4N32	4N32	4N32	7B38	7 38	8 48	8 48	1235	2 24	2†33	3 30	6 48	8 45
—	Inverness dep.	6 5	6 42	7 25	9 20	9 48	1015	1025	2 40	4 15	5 0	6 5	8 15	1040
3½	Bunchrew	..	..	..	9 30	..	..	1035	2 50	J	5 10	6 14	8 25	1050
5½	Lentran	..	X	..	9 35	..	..	1041	2 55	..	5 15	6 19	8 30	1055
7¼	Clunes	6 20	..	..	9 38	..	1029	..	2 59	..	5 19	6 22	8 34	1059
9¾	Beauly	6 26	7 4	7 42	9 44	10 5	1035	1048	3 8	..	5 26	6 28	8 40	11 5
12¾	Muir of Ord Jnc. 751	6 34	..	7 51	9 56	..	..	1055	3 18	..	5 34	6 35	8 47	1112
16	Conon	6 42	..	..	10 5	..	1047	..	3 26	..	5 41	6 42	8 59	1119
18½	Dingwall arr.	6 48	7 21	8 2	1011	1025	1053	11 7	3 33	4 46	5 47	6 48	9 5	1125
	748, 751 dep.	6 55	7 23	The Hebridean. Restaurant Car, Inverness to Kyle of Lochalsh, page 748.	1014	1030	Restaurant Car, Inverness to Kyle of Lochalsh, page 748. The Lewisman.	1112	3 36	4 48	5 50	6 49	9 8	
22¾	Foulis	7 1	..		1022	..		..	3 43	..	5 58	6 57	9 16	Saturdays only.
24¾	Novar	7 8	..		1028	1042		1124	3 49	..	6 4	7 3	9 22	
28¼	Alness	7 16	..		1035	1050		1132	3 57	..	6 11	7 10	9 29	
31¼	Invergordon	7 23	7 44		1042	11 0		1139	4 6	..	6 21	7 17	9 36	
34¾	Delny	7 31	..		1051	..		..	4 12	..	6 28	7 24	9 43	
36½	Kildary	7 36	..		1056	1112		1150	4 18	..	6 33	7 29	9 48	
39	Nigg	7 41	..		11 2	..		..	4 25	..	6 38	7 34	9 53	
40½	Fearn	7 45	..		11 6	1120		1158	4 30	..	6 42	7 38	9 57	
44	Tain arr.	7 56	8 10		1115	1128		12 7	4 39	5 26	6 50	7 46	10 5	
	dep.	Stop	8 20		..	1130		1210	4 45	5 30	..	..	..	..
49¼	Edderton		8 30		..	1140		1222	4 55	..	..	..	..	..
57½	Bonar Bridge arr.	..	8 45		..	1155		1238	5 10	5 50	..	..	..	..
	dep.	..	8 48		..	1156		1242	5 12	5 52	..	..	..	..
60½	Culrain	..	8A55		..	12 2		1249	5 20	..	..	..	..	..
61	Invershin	..	8 59		..	12 5		1251	5 25	..	..	..	..	..
66½	Lairg	..	9 15		..	1220		1 9	5 40	Aa	..	..	..	..
76½	Rogart	..	9 38		..	Commences 24th inst.		1 32	6 0	6 38	..	..	..	..
80½	The Mound Jnc. 751	..	9 48		..			1 41	6 8	6 49	..	..	..	..
84	Golspie	..	10 0		..			1 50	6 18	6 56	..	..	..	..
86	Dunrobin (Private)	..	10A6		..			..	6A25	..	..	..	..	..
90¼	Brora	..	1017		..			2 5	6 35	7 9	..	..	..	..
95½	Loth	..	1027		..			2 15	6 45	..	..	..	..	..
101¼	Helmsdale	..	1043		..			2 30	6 56	7 26	..	..	..	..
104½	Salzcraggie Platform	..	1054A		..	..		..	Stop	..	..	..	..	..
110¾	Kildonan	..	11 8	..	..	..		2 50		..	..	..	..	..
113½	Borrobol Platform	..	1116A	..	..	..		..	..	..	..	..	..	..
118	Kinbrace	..	1130	..	..	..		3A 8	..	..	..	..	..	..
125½	Forsinard	..	1145	..	..	..		3 24	..	..	..	..	..	..
133¾	Altnabreac	..	12 2	..	..	..		3A38	..	..	..	..	..	..
142¾	Scotscalder	..	1216	..	..	..		3A50	..	..	..	..	..	..
145½	Halkirk	..	1222	..	..	..		3 57	..	..	..	..	..	..
147	Georgemas arr.	mrn	1227	..	..	..		4 1	aft	8 46	..	..	..	..
	Junc. 751 dep.	1035	1232	..	..	..		4 6	5 22	8 49	..	..	..	..
149¾	Bower	1042	12 5A	..	..	..	..	Kk	5 27	..	..	..	..	..
153¾	Watten	1055	1240	..	..	..	..	4 18	5 35	..	..	..	..	..
156	Bilbster	11 3	1245	..	..	..	..	..	5 41	..	..	..	..	..
161¼	Wick 751 arr.	11 8	1254	..	..	..	..	4 29	5 51	9 10	..	..	..	..

Up.	Week Days.														Sn
	mrn	mrn	mrn	aft	aft	Z	aft	J	mrn	aft	aft	H	aft	aft	aft
Wick dep.	..	..	..	..	..	8 45	..	1010	1135	..	..	3 40	6 45	1015	..
Bilbster	..	..	..	..	..	8 53	..	..	1145	..	..	3 48	6 54	1024	..
Watten	..	..	..	..	..	8 58	..	..	1155	..	..	3 53	7 0	1030	..
Bower	..	..	..	..	..	9 4	..	..	1210	..	..	3 59	7 6	..	..
Georgemas arr.	..	..	..	..	..	9 10	..	1030	1225	..	..	4 5	7 14	1042	..
Junc. 751 dep.	..	..	..	..	..	9 15	..	1035	Stop	..	Restaurant Car, Kyle of Lochalsh to Inverness, page 748.	4 10	Stop		..
Halkirk	Thro Carrs, Kyle of Lochalsh to Glasgow, pages 748 and 747. The Lewisman.	..	..	Restaurant Car, Kyle of Lochalsh to Inverness, page 748. The Hebridean.	..	9 19	..	..		..		4 14		Saturdays only.	..
Scotscalder		..	..		..	9 25	..	..	..	..		4 20	..		..
Altnabreac		..	..		..	9A40	..	..	..	..		4A35	..		..
Forsinard		..	..		..	10 1	..	..	..	..		4 54	..		..
Kinbrace		..	..		..	1015	..	1128	..	..		5 8	..		..
Borrobol Platform		..	..			A1020	..	..	..	..		5A12	..		..
Kildonan		..	..		..	1030	..	..	..	..		5 21	..		..
Salzcraggie Platform		..	..			A1040	..	..	..	..		5A30	..		..
Helmsdale		..	6 10		..	1050	..	12 5	..	..		5 45	..		..
Loth		..	..		..	11 2	..	..	..	..		5 56	..		..
Brora		..	6 28		..	1113	..	1225	..	..		6 6	..	..	..
Dunrobin (Private)		..	6A33			A1119	..	..	..	..		6A12	..	..	..
Golspie		..	6 42		..	1123	..	1237	..	..		6 20	..	..	..
The Mound Jnc. 751		..	6 49		..	1140	..	..	..	..		6 29	..	..	..
Rogart		..	6 56		..	1151	..	..	..	..		6 39	..	..	..
Lairg		..	7 22		..	1217	..	1 13	..	..		7 2	..	..	1 0
Invershin		..	7 32		..	1229	..	..	..	..		7 13	..	..	1 10
Culrain		..	7 35		..	1232	..	..	..	..		7A15	..	..	1 13
Bonar Bridge arr.		..	7 42		..	1239	..	1 30	..	..		7 22	..	..	1 21
dep.		..	7 44		..	1245	..	1 31	..	..		7 24	..	..	1 22
Edderton		..	7 58		..	1 0	..	..	..	..		7 38	..	..	..
Tain arr.		..	8 11		..	1 11	..	1 52	..	..		7 48	aft	..	1 46
dep.		..	8 20		1240	1 18	130	1 55	..	4 0		7 50	8 5	..	1 50
Fearn		..	8 30		1247	..	136	..	..	4 6		The Orcadian.	8 11	..	1 59
Nigg		..	8 37		1251	..	140	..	..	4 10			8 15	..	..
Kildary		..	8 43		1257	..	145	..	..	4 17			8 20	..	2 10
Delny		..	8 48		1 1	..	150	..	aft	4 22			8 24	..	..
Invergordon		..	8 57		1 11	1 45	158	2 19	2 30	4 30			8 32	..	2 22
Alness		..	9 5		1 20	..	..	..	2 36	4 36			8 38	..	2 31
Novar		..	9 14		1 28	..	..	..	2 42	4 44			8 44	..	2 39
Foulis		..	9 22		1 35	..	..	..	2 48	4 48			8 50	..	..
Dingwall arr.		..	9 32		1 46	2 8	..	2 40	2 57	5 1		8 33	8 59	..	2 54
748, 751 dep.	7 22	8 5	9 42	1 40	1 50	2 14	..	2 42	3 0	5 5	820	8 40	9 6	..	2 57
Conon	..	8 10	9 48	..	1 55	..	..	..	3 5	5 10	827	..	9 11	..	3 3
Muir of Ord Jnc. 751	7 33	8 18	9 56	1 52	2 2	..	..	..	3 14	5 18	835	..	9 19	..	3 10
Beauly	7 42	8 24	10 6	..	2 8	..	..	..	3 25	5 26	840	..	9 25	..	3 16
Clunes	..	8 30	1015	..	2 15	..	..	..	3 30	5 32	..	..	9A30	..	..
Lentran	..	8 35	1020A		2 20	..	..	..	3 37	5 38	..	..	9A34	..	..
Bunchrew	..	8 41	1023A		2 25	..	..	..	3 42	5 43	..	..	9A38	..	..
Inverness 747 .. arr.	8 10	8 53	1042	2 20	2 33	3 0	..	3 20	3 54	5 54	9 6	9 17	9 50	—	3 41
747 AVIEMORE .. arr.	9 33	1211	1218	4 25	4 25	4 25	..	4 48	5 47	9S30	..	1C0	1C0	..	5 14
747 PERTH (Gen). "	1151	..	2 56	7 0	7 0	7 0	..	7 20	8 46	1213	S	4C20	4C20	..	7 45

A Stops when required. Aa Stops at 6 25 aft. when required to set down from South of Inverness. B Restaurant Car Inverness to Helmsdale. Through Carriage, Inverness to Thurso, page 751. B Except 6th inst. C Except Sunday morn. H Restaurant Car, Helmsdale to Inverness. Thro Carriage, Thurso to Inverness, page 751. J The John o'Groat Restaurant Car between Inverness and Wick. Kk Stops at 4 10 aft. to set down from Forsinard and South thereof on notice being given at Georgemas Junction. N Dep. Perth 12 55 and Aviemore 3 23 mrn on Mons. P Through Carriage Glasgow to Wick, page 746. Restaurant Car, Inverness to The Mound Junction. Through Carriage, Inverness to Thurso, page 751. S Sats. only. † Dep. Perth 12 5 and Aviemore 2 37 aft. on Fris. and Sats. X The Orcadian. Z Thro Carrs., Thurso to Inverness (page 751) and Wick to Glasgow (page 747.) Restaurant Car, The Mound Junc. to Inverness.

Train Services

The initial service to Dingwall consisted of four trains each way daily, one of which was mixed. An omnibus ran to and from Strathpeffer in connection with most trains, but this was not mentioned in adverts after the first few months. Messrs Wordie & Co. were appointed agents to handle parcels and goods at Beauly and Dingwall. A Sunday mail train was added in 1863. Coach connections were also provided northwards from Dingwall. As sections opened, these trains were extended and the coach journeys reduced. The journey to Bonar Bridge took about 3 hours. Winter traffic does not seem to have justified this level of service, as the January 1865 timetable shows only two trains to Bonar Bridge and a third as far as Tain. The Sunday train only ran to Tain. Four trains ran through to Bonar Bridge in the summer months and the following winter three trains went that far, with a fourth to Tain. The Sunday train, which would have been run for mail traffic, continued to Bonar Bridge.

The opening of the Dingwall & Skye Railway on 19th August 1870 brought additional traffic to the section south of Dingwall, mainly during the summer. In winter, traffic to Strome Ferry was light; in the first few years one train each way sufficed in winter and two in summer, all connecting at Dingwall with Inverness trains. In later years, some of the Skye line trains ran through independently between Inverness and Dingwall.

Once the line was completed to Wick, the service settled down to two passenger trains throughout. Even then, one of the southbound trains was mixed and set off at 12.10am. A further train ran each way as far as Helmsdale plus one only as far as Tain. There was a single mail train on Sundays. Journey time from Inverness to

INVERNESS & ABERDEEN JUNCTION RAILWAY.

O P E N I N G

OF THE INVERNESS AND ROSS-SHIRE LINE FROM INVERNESS TO DINGWALL.

THE Public are respectfully informed that on *Wednesday, 11th June* 1862, and until further notice, the TRAINS will ARRIVE and DEPART at the following hours, or as near thereto as circumstances will admit, viz. :—

UP TRAINS.

	1	2	3 Mixed.	4	
	A.M.	P.M.	P.M.	P.M.	
Dingwall, depart	8·40	12·0	4·0	7·20	
Conon ,,	8·48	12·8	4·10	7·28	
Tarradale ,,	8·59	12·18	4·22	7.38	
Beauly ,,	9·10	12·28	4·38	7·47	
Lentran ,,	9·22	12·40	4·50	7·59	
Bunchrew ,,	9·29	12·47	4·58	8·6	
Inverness, arrive	9·40	1·0	5·10	8·20	
Inverness depart	10·5	3·15	5·30	6·40 A	
Nairn ,,	10·47	4·0	6·18	7·15	
Forres ,,	11·16	4·28	6·52	7·37	
Elgin ,,	11·55	5·11	7·40	8·3	
Fochabers ,,	12·17 P	5·32	8·20	8·24	
Keith, arrive	12·55	6·7	9·10	9·0	
Keith, depart	1·0	6·15	—	9·10	10·5
Aberdeen { arrive, G.N.S.	3·45	9·0	—	11·55	1·5 P
Aberdeen { depart, S.N.E.	4·15	6.0 A	—	12·23 P	—
Perth, arrive	7·15	10·30	—	3·48	—
Edinburgh, per E.P. & D. arrive	9·40	1·15 P	—	—	—
Edinburgh, per S.C	10·0	2·0	—	6·20	—
Glasgow, per S.C.	9·45	1·40	—	6·15	—
London, per G.N.	9·40 A	3·30 A	—	—	—
Do. per L. & N.W.	9·40	6·0	—	4·37	—

DOWN TRAINS.

	1	2	3	4
	A.M.	A.M.	A.M.	P.M.
London, per L. & N. W. depart	—	—	9·0	8·40
Do. per G.N. ,,	—	—	9·0	—
Glasgow, per S.C. depart	—	—	8·40 P	6·40 A
Edinburgh, ,, ,,	—	—	8·15	6·25
Do. per E.P. & D. ,,	—	—	6·0	6·0
Perth ,,	—	—	11·40	9·20
Aberdeen { arr. per S.N.E.	—	—	3·0 A	12·35 P
Aberdeen { dep. per G.N.S.	—	—	8·0	1·20
Keith, arrive	—	—	10·51	3.57
Keith, depart	—	7·0	11·0	4·5
Fochabers, depart	—	7·39	11·37	4·46
Elgin ,,	—	8·5	12·0 P	5·13
Forres ,,	—	8·40	12·36	5·52
Nairn ,,	—	9·6	1·1	6·18
Inverness, arrive	—	9·50	1·45	7·0
	Mixed			
Inverness, depart	8·30	10·30	4·5	7·15
Bunchrew ,,	8·42	10·44	4·19	7·29
Lentran ,,	8·51	10·52	4·26	7·36
Beauly ,,	9·10	11.4	4·38	7·47
Tarradale ,,	9·22	11·14	4·48	7·57
Conon ,,	9·32	11·24	4·58	8·7
Dingwall ,,	9·40	11·30	5·5	8·15

For Passenger Fares, Conditions under which Tickets are issued, Goods Trains, &c., see the Company's Time Tables.

The Agents at the respective Stations will give information as to Rates for the conveyance of Goods, Live Stock, &c.

By order.

AND. DOUGALL, *General Manager.*

Inverness, 10th June 1862.

INVERNESS & ABERDEEN JUNCTION RAILWAY.

ON 23d March 1863, and until further notice, the Trains will Arrive and Depart at the following hours, of as near thereto as circumstances will permit:—

Time taken from the Railway Clocks.

UP TRAINS.

STATIONS.	1 Fast Mail Class 1 and 3	2 Parl. Class 1 & 3	3 Pass. Class 1 & 3	4 Mix. Class 1 & 3	5 Pass. Class 1 & 3
	A.M.	A.M.	P.M.	P.M.	P.M.
Invergordon ....dep.	—	7.50	10.50	3.20	6.40
Alness .... ,,	—	8.0	11.0	3.30	6.50
Novar .... ,,	—	8.10	11.10	3.40	7.0
Fowlis .... ,,	—	8.17	11.17	3.47	7.7
Dingwall .... ,,	—	8.30	11.30	4.0	7.20
Conon .... ,,	—	8.38	11.38	4.10	7.28
Muir of Ord .... ,,	—	8.49	11.48	4.22	7.38
Beauly .... ,,	—	9.0	11.58	4.38	7.47
Lentran .... ,,	—	9.12	12.10	4.50	7.59
Bunchrew .... ,,	—	9.19	12.18	4.58	8.6
Inverness ....arr.	—	9.30	12.30	5.10	8.20
Inverness ....dep.	6.40	10.5	3.15	5.35	—
Culloden .... ,,	—	10.14	3.25	5.45	—
Dalcross .... ,,	—	10.24	3.35	5.55	—
Fort-George .... ,,	7.2	10.32	3.44	6.5	—
Nairn .... ,,	7.15	10.47	4.0	6.21	—
Brodie .... ,,	7.28	11.3	4.16	6.40	—
Forres .... ,,	7.37	11.16	4.28	6.52	—
Kinloss .... ,,	—	11.25	4.38	7.0	—
Findhorn .... arr.	—	11.58	4.58	7.20	—
Findhorn .... dep.	—	11.0	—	—	—
Alves .... ,,	7.50	11.37	4.50	7.14	—
Burghead .... arr.	8.45	12.40	5.55	—	—
Burghead .... dep.	7.25	11.10	4.25	—	—
Elgin .... arr.	8.1	11.52	5.6	7.34	—
Elgin .... dep.	8.3	11.55	5.11	7.40	—
		P.M.			
Lhanbryde .... ,,	8.14	12.5	5.22	7.54	—
Fochabers .... ,,	8.24	12.17	5.32	8.20	—
Orton .... ,,	8.35	12.29	5.42	8.31	—
Mulben .... ,,	8.48	12.42	5.54	8.51	—
Keith ....arr.	9.0	12.55	6.7	9.10	—
Keith ....dep.	9.10 10.5	1.0	6.15	—	—
Aberdeen ....arr.	11.55 1.5	3.45	9.0	—	—
	P.M.				
Edinburgh, per S.C. ...arr.	6.20 —	9.55	1.10	—	—
Do. per E. P. & D.	9.45 —	—	1.5	—	—
Glasgow, per S.C.	6.15 —	9.45	1.15	—	—
	A.M.	A.M.	A.M.		
London, *via* G.N.	— —	9.40	3.30	—	—
London, *via* L. & N.W.	4.37 —	9.40	6.0	—	—

Timetable published in the Inverness Courier.

DOWN TRAINS.

STATIONS.	1 Mix. Class 1 & 3	2 Pass Class 1 & 3	3 Pass. Class 1 & 3	4 Mix. Class 1 & 3	5 Parl. Mail 1 & 3	6 Pass. Class 1 & 3
	A.M.	A.M.	A.M.	P.M.	P.M.	P.M.
London, *via* L. & N.W. dep.	—	—	10·0	—	8.40	9.15
London, *via* G.N.	—	—	10.0	—	—	9.15
			P.M.		A.M.	A.M.
Glasgow, per E. & G.	—	—	9.10	—	6.40	9 30
Edinburgh, Do.	—	—	8.45	—	6.25	9.15
Do., per E. P. & D.	—	—	6.15	—	6.15	9.40
			A.M.		P.M.	P.M.
Aberdeen ....dep.	—	—	8.0	—	1.20	4.40
Keith ....arr.	—	—	10.51	—	3.57	7.20
Keith ....dep.	—	7.0	11.0	—	4.5	7.40
Mulben .... ,,	—	7.14	11.13	—	4.19	7.54
Orton .... ,,	—	7.29	11.28	—	4.35	8.8
Fochabers .... ,,	—	7.39	11.37	—	4.46	8.20
Lhanbryde .... ,,	—	7.49	11.46	—	4.59	8.30
Elgin .... arr.	—	8.0	11.55	—	5.8	8.40
			P.M.			
Elgin .... dep.	—	8.5	12.0	1.40	5.13	8.43
Burghead .... arr.	—	8.45	12.40	—	5.55	—
Burghead .... dep.	—	7.25	11.10	—	4.25	—
Alves .... ,,	—	8.20	12.14	2.10	5.28	8.56
Kinloss .... ,,	—	8.31	12.26	2.30	5.40	9.7
Findhorn .... arr.	—	—	—	—	—	—
Findhorn .... dep.	—	—	11.0	2.0	5.22	—
Forres .... ,,	—	8.40	12.36	3.0	5.52	9.15
Brodie .... ,,	—	8.51	12.46	3.25	6.2	9.25
Nairn .... ,,	—	9.6	1.1	4.0	6.21	9.39
Fort-George .... ,,	—	9.21	1.16	4.25	6.33	9.52
Dalcross .... ,,	—	9.30	1.25	4.35	6.41	—
Culloden .... ,,	—	9.40	1.35	4.48	6.50	—
Inverness ....arr.	—	9.50	1.45	5.0	7.0	10.15
Inverness ....dep.	8.20	10.30	4.5	—	7.15	—
Bunchrew .... ,,	8.32	10.44	4.19	—	7.29	—
Lentran .... ,,	8.41	10.52	4.26	—	7.36	—
Beauly .... ,,	9.0	11.4	4.38	—	7.47	—
Muir of Ord .... ,,	9.12	11.14	4.48	—	7.57	—
Conon .... ,,	9.22	11.24	4.58	—	8.7	—
Dingwall .... ,,	9 30	11.30	5.5	—	8.15	—
Fowlis .... ,,	9.43	11.43	5.18	—	8.28	—
Novar .... ,,	9.50	11.50	5.25	—	8.35	—
Alness .... ,,	10.0	12.0	5.35	—	8.45	—
Invergordon .... ,,	10.10	12.10	5.45	—	8.55	—

RETURN TICKETS are issued Daily, except Sunday, by all the Trains, from any Station to any other Station, available for returning by any Train same day, and on Saturdays at One Ordinary Fare, available to return same day or the following Monday. For Fares, &c., see small bills.

Composition Tickets are granted to all the Stations on moderate terms, which may be learned on application at any of the Company's Offices.

Fisherwomen with their burdens will get 3rd Class Tickots at Burghead for Elgin, Forres, Keith, and Inverness, at the following Fares, viz.:—To Elgin and back same day, 1s.; to Forres and back same day, 1s. 2d.; to Keith and back same day, 2s. 6d.; to Inverness and back same day, 3s. 6d.

An Omnibus runs between Fochabers and the Fochabers Station, in connection with most of the Trains. For Hours see small bills.

The Arrangements of other Railways, Coaches, &c., are inserted for the convenience of Passengers, but this Company will not be responsible for their correctness.

PARCELS BY PASSENGER TRAINS.—Parcels will be conveyed by all the Passenger Trains, and will be received at the Company's Offices, up to Fifteen Minutes before the time appointed for the departure of the respective Trains.

GOODS TRAFFIC.—Merchandise and Live Stock will be conveyed by the Trains leaving Inverness at 6.15 P.M., and Keith at 11.15 A.M. Messrs Wordie & Co., Sole Agents for the Company, receive and deliver Goods and Parcels in Dingwall, Beauly, Inverness, Nairn, Forres, Elgin, Garmouth, and Keith.

☞ Horses and Carriages carried by all the Trains.

By Order.

AND. DOUGALL, *General-Manager.*

Inverness & Aberdeen Junction Railway Office,
Inverness, 23d March 1863.

The carriage of newspapers was an important traffic until the 1980s. The Highland Railway issued perforated stamps for small bundles of newspapers, but they had to be open at each end. Still, the rate was very reasonable. This example was printed on a light buff paper and was produced before 1884 as the line north of Bonar Bridge was owned by a separate company until then. (John Roake colln)

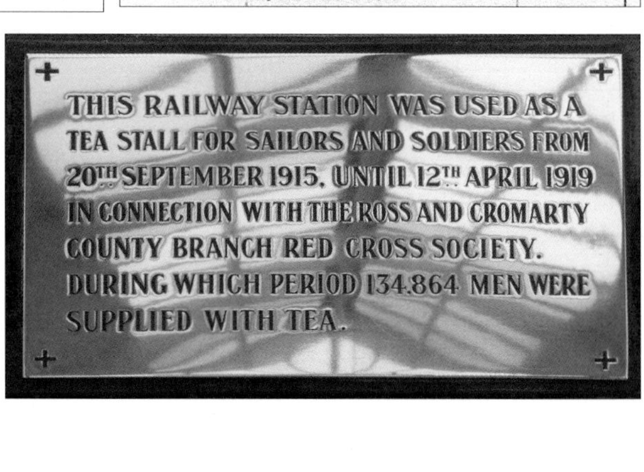

This plaque at Dingwall records the contribution made by the local Red Cross Society members during the last War. (Jack Kernahan)

Most of the Kyle of Lochalsh trains ran through to and from Inverness, but Strathpeffer branch trains nearly always ran only as far as Dingwall, with connections there for Inverness. Here passengers are transferring from a train from Inverness hauled by No.7 Ben Attow *on the left to the branch train sitting in the north bay on the right. That is hauled by Passenger Tank No.25, at that time appropriately named* Strathpeffer. *It was Highland Railway practice to name branch locomotives after the line on which they ran.* *(John Roake collection)*

Bonar Bridge was around 3 hours. In 1885, there was a general speeding up of trains south of Inverness triggered by the Post Office, which wanted faster delivery of mail. This rippled through to changes north of Inverness, although those services were little faster.

By 1900, the up overnight train had been replaced by a daytime one and with some extra workings to Tain, this remained the basic pattern until the 1960s. In the summer of 1906, the Further North Express was introduced. It ran weekly and arrangements changed from year to year. Initially, it operated on Fridays northbound, running non-stop to The Mound and then on to Dornoch, and there was no return working. That winter, it was altered to run to Wick and stops included Dingwall, Tain and Bonar Bridge. Although it missed most of the stations, at 2 hours the time to Bonar Bridge was only 15 minutes less than the mail train. An up working on Thursdays was added. This round-the-year service continued until 1912, when the winter train was withdrawn but in the summer of 1913 and 1914 it ran northbound on Wednesdays and Fridays, southbound on Thursdays and Saturdays. The LMS re-introduced this train in 1923 in the northbound direction, but this time starting at Aviemore and running non-stop to Dingwall in 95 minutes. The following season, it ran from Inverness, northbound on Friday and southbound on Saturday. By 1936 it was running daily.

Another interesting train over the line was the Strathpeffer Spa Express, introduced in 1911 to serve the new hotel at Strathpeffer. This ran on Tuesdays only from Aviemore, where it connected with a train from Perth, direct to Dingwall without stopping at Inverness. Arrangements varied slightly over the next three seasons and it was even advertised in 1915, but appears not to have operated that year. Nor did it run after the War.

Sunday trains continued until 1920 when the Post Office withdrew Sunday deliveries. In the 1930s, a train carrying newspapers northbound to Lairg was introduced on Sundays; the return working carried passengers.

As well as introducing more modern carriages, the LMS also provided restaurant cars on many of the trains going through to Wick and Kyle of Lochalsh.

The Bens were introduced in 1898 to work the main trains on the less hilly routes north and east of Inverness. By 1946 they were seeing out their days on light work, such as this single coach train to Fortrose getting away from Muir of Ord. The locomotive is No.14406 Ben Slioch.

When the diesel locomotives introduced in the early 1960s came to the end of their working lives, Class 37s were transferred to Inverness to work the Far North and Kyle lines. With their 6-wheel bogies, these were a bit harsh on the track. New coaches also came north in the early 1980s when Mark II carriages from the late 1960s replaced the Mark I vehicles built in the 1950s and early 1960s. No.37 419 heads a mixed rake of Mark I and Mark II carriages on a northbound train at Fearn. (John Roake collection)

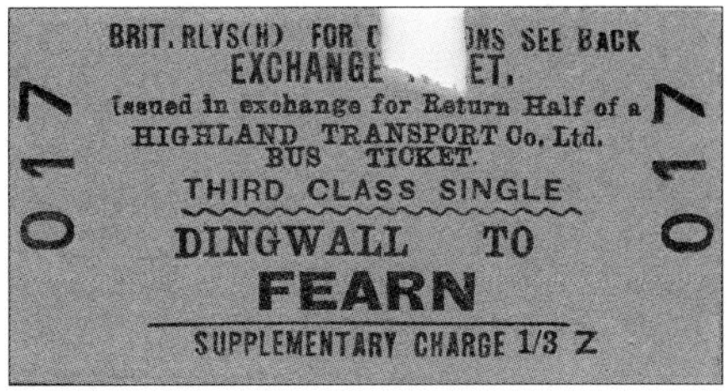

While competing bus services drew much of the local traffic from the railway, there were occasions when holders of bus tickets wanted to travel by train. They could do so on payment of the difference and were issued with exchange tickets such as this. (John Roake collection)

After the War, the basic train service returned. The pattern of operation was quite complex, with coaches being added and removed at intermediate points such as Dingwall. For instance, the first train set out from Inverness about 7am, where it connected with the overnight train from Glasgow and Edinburgh. It could load to 20 vehicles as far as Dingwall, about half of which carried parcel traffic. Four of these vehicles would be detached at Dingwall to form part of a freight train to Kyle. The rest of the train, including an ex-Pullman restaurant car serving breakfast, would continue north to Wick and Thurso, but station stops were lengthy as parcels and mail was dropped off. The Tain locals were shorter and self-contained, generally consisting of three coaches, a couple of brake thirds and a composite, plus the odd van when traffic warranted.

In the early 1950s, coal shortages led to the withdrawal of one of the Tain locals and this was never restored. Some of the smaller stations were not served by all trains. Foulis, for instance, only had a couple; a return journey could not be made there in a day from the south, although cheap day return tickets were advertised! Then the closures of June 1960 resulted in the withdrawal of the Tain locals. All that was left were the two trains to Wick and one to Helmsdale, this being extended to Wick in the peak summer months, plus two or three Kyle trains to Dingwall. These were, however, faster. In September 1964, the timetable was recast so that all three trains ran through to and from Wick and this remained the service until recent years. The Sunday train to Lairg continued and eventually passengers were allowed on the northbound run but this ceased when newspaper transport by rail stopped in the early 1980s.

A freight train from Inverness entering Dingwall in June 1949 hauled by Stanier Black Five No.45128. There were several vans for parcels traffic. *(J L Stevenson)*

Regular Sunday trains through to Wick and Thurso began operating after the introduction of radio signalling.

With the development of Inverness over the last few years has come an increase in travel from places to the north and increased road congestion. This has encouraged commuting into Inverness. To meet this demand, the service over the line has been greatly improved, particularly south of Tain. Local trains once again operate to supplement the through trains which have increased to four daily, plus one on Sundays. Three trains now arrive at Inverness before 9am and measures have had to be taken to reduce overcrowding on the return trains in the evening.

Mail had always been an important traffic and the contract with the GPO made a significant contribution to the Company's balance sheet. In most cases mail was carried in the guard's van and handed to or from GPO staff at each station. With its long run, a travelling post office was introduced between Perth and Inverness by 1870 and this was extended to Bonar Bridge by 1876. Sorting tenders, later sorting carriages, ran on both the night and day trains to a pattern which varied over the years. Their times were dictated by the GPO and ensured that mail posted by early evening in London reached stations north of Inverness the following day.

By 1930, a single carriage operated. This left Perth about 6am, after connecting with the Down Special TPO from London the previous evening, was transferred at Inverness to the 10.30am Kyle train and then dropped off at Dingwall where the sorting staff completed their shift. Another Post Office employee worked on the vehicle as it was attached to the following Wick train which took it to Helmsdale. The vehicle returned south on the early morning train from Helmsdale and was dropped off at Dingwall about 9.30am where it remained until about 2pm when it was attached to the first southbound train from Wick. It was transferred at Inverness to a southbound train to continue its journey to Perth. The TPO ceased north of Inverness on 8th August 1970.

A northbound freight, headed by a Class 24, was shunting at Muir of Ord in August 1969 when the morning passenger to Kyle passed by. Wagonload freight was still the norm. *(Keith Fenwick)*

Where the train did not stop, apparatus for picking up and dropping off mail was provided. These appears to have been used until the late 1930s. The locations listed in 1898, all equipped with one net and one standard on the down (west) side of the line, were :

Clunes	300 yards north of station
Muir of Ord	220 yards north of station
Conon Bridge	300 yards south of station
Delny	300 yards north of station
Nigg	Close to south end of station

While freight was initially carried in mixed trains, it became necessary to run separate trains after continuous brakes were introduced to comply with the Regulation of Railways Act 1889. As well as a through train to Wick, shorter workings were introduced. In 1922, there were three each way daily north of Bonar Bridge, another to Tain and one to Dingwall. In the late 1940s, there were freight trains from Inverness at 5.15am to Wick, 5.45 to Helmsdale, 6.40 to Kyle of Lochalsh, 9.40 to Tain, 10.45 to Dingwall, 1.25pm to Helmsdale and 3pm to Dingwall. The stopping pattern varied, with the longer-distance trains missing out many of the station nearer Inverness. The southbound pattern was similar. If fish landings at Wick were good, a separate train would be run at 4.10pm, but otherwise a couple of fish wagons could be attached to the front of the preceding passenger train at 3.30pm.

At that time, collection and delivery was available from Beauly, Muir of Ord, Dingwall, Alness, Invergordon, Tain and Bonar Bridge. The road vehicles involved would also visit some of the other stations to perform local delivery. As the capacity of road vehicles increased, it became more practical and economic to cover a larger area from the main stations and the role of the minor ones decreased. Special trains, for instance for the autumn sheep sales, continued to operate but by the late 1950s, this traffic died away.

Since then, it has been a story of gradual reduction, with a brief surge in the 1970s mainly to the Invergordon area, until freight completely ceased in the 1980s. The grain silo at Muir of Ord required a regular working during the 1970s and early 1980s. Over the last few years, some traffic has been gained, but not much has lasted and none has been to stations south of Bonar Bridge. Sidings remained at many stations long after traffic to them ceased, but nearly all have now been disconnected.

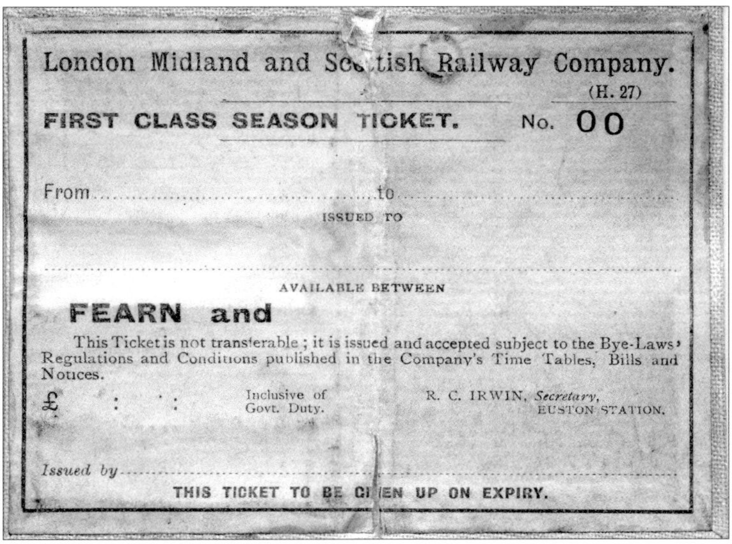
London Midland and Sc[illegible]tish Railway Company.
(H. 27)
FIRST CLASS SEASON TICKET. No. 00
From .... to ....
ISSUED TO
AVAILABLE BETWEEN
FEARN and
This Ticket is not transferable ; it is issued and accepted subject to the Bye-Laws, Regulations and Conditions published in the Company's Time Tables, Bills and Notices.
£ : : Inclusive of Govt. Duty. R. C. IRWIN, Secretary, EUSTON STATION.
Issued by ....
THIS TICKET TO BE G[illegible]EN UP ON EXPIRY.

While there were a few regular travellers from stations such as Fearn, there may not have been many in First Class.
(John Roake collection)

In its early days, the I&AJ obtained several 2-2-2 locomotives. Their single drivers were not much suited to the hills of the Perth line but they did manage the more level line north from Inverness. No. 32 Cluny, *one of the Glenbarry class was built in 1864 and originally called* Sutherland. *It was renamed* Cluny *in 1874 and in this condition was photographed at Dingwall. It remained a 2-2-2 until withdrawal in 1898, although several others of the same design were rebuilt as 2-4-0s, including no.55 which was built in 1864 and originally called* Cluny. *It became a 2-4-0 in 1874, when it took the name* Sutherland, *changed in turn to* Invergordon *in 1884. Another of the class was named* Dingwall.

One of the early locomotives known to have operated on the line north of Inverness was Raigmore class 2-4-0 No.2 in its form as rebuilt in 1871. It is seen here in its later days at Inverness. (HRS collection)

Locomotives and Rolling Stock

Nearly all the Highland Railway locomotive classes saw service on the line at one time or another. Some went new to the Far North line, but most were moved there from the Perth line when replaced by newer stock. The I&AJ initially relied on a fleet of 2-2-2 and 2-4-0 classes, all very light in design. For the opening to Dingwall in 1862, two more 2-4-0 goods engines of the existing 14 class were purchased but for passenger trains a development of the Raigmore class 2-2-2s was obtained from Hawthorns of Leith. The first, No.13, was named *Belladrum* after the residence of James Merry, a director, and this gave the name to the class. The second loco, No.14, was named *Lovat*. Over the next few years, various 2-4-0s and 4-4-0s were to be seen on the line. When Peter Drummond took over as Locomotive Engineer in 1896, there was an urgent need to replace some of the older locomotives, so his first design, the Small Ben, was intended for the easier runs north and east of Inverness. Similarly, the Highland's only 0-6-0 tender class, the Barney, was particularly at home on these lines. In 1913, the Castle class 4-6-0s started appearing on the line but the track was not really up to the operation of 6-coupled locos at the time.

The huge traffic demands of the First World War saw the Highland's locomotive stock severely stretched, partly because regular maintenance could not be carried out properly. The Bens could not handle the main Wick mail trains, so two new 4-4-0s, *Snaigow* and *Durn* were built in 1916. That hardly met the general need for more motive power, so the Company appealed to other railways for help and was lent a variety of locomotives, many quite elderly; some remained in the north until the early 1920s. Only occasional details of what was actually in use have survived. For instance, a North Eastern Railway BTP class 0-4-4T was photographed off the rails at Dingwall in 1921 and a London & South Western Adams 4-4-2T appears in a photograph at Fortrose in 1919. A Great North of Scotland 4-4-0 reached Invergordon with a train of coal. The strangest incomer was a Great Western steam rail motor, which was on loan from January 1918 to March 1924 and is known to have worked in the Invergordon area.

The LMS provided newer engines for the Perth line and continued the practice of transferring older locomotives north of Inverness so Highland classes were the mainstay until the Second World War, when Stanier Class 5s were needed as once again traffic was very heavy; known to enthusiasts as Black Fives, they were referred to as Hikers by local railwaymen. Stanier Class 8 2-8-0s, which were used on the Perth line, made at least one trip on the Far North line. By the early 1950s, nearly all the Highland engines had been withdrawn. Black Fives and Caledonian 4-4-0s generally powered the trains until diesels took over in 1960/61. For many years these were type 2s, of what later became classes 24, 25, 26 and 27 but in the 1980s, they were replaced by Class 37s. Class 20s appeared on freight workings in the 1960s and 70s.

Locomotive depots were established at Dingwall and Tain until the change to diesel traction and the withdrawal of the Tain locals so they closed in 1961 and 1960 respectively. Nowadays, the stock is based at Inverness where comprehensive service facilities have been developed.

Coaching stock in early years was 4-wheeled, all non-corridor without any conveniences

A portent of things to come. In 1958, two years before diesels arrived to take over, D5511 spent several days on test in the Highlands. It is seen here arriving at Tain, while Black Five 45483 waits with a southbound train. *(John Roake collection)*

and no heating apart from footwarmers for first class passengers. Lighting was by oil lamp. Improvements came gradually, being introduced usually on the line south to Perth first. Six wheelers replaced 4-wheeled coaches and then in the early years of the twentieth century gas lighting and lavatories were provided in some of the coaches used on the through trains. Steam heating was in general use throughout the country before being introduced on the Far North line in 1911/12. Electric lighting came in about then as well and bogie coaches made their appearance, but local trains remained with older coaches for many years more. The LMS made significant changes soon after it took over, introducing dining cars on the Wick trains as well as more corridor coaches. Six-wheeled coaches disappeared, even though the local trains were still non-corridor with no lavatories. That was the norm for those days and persisted until the trains were withdrawn.

British Railways Mark I coaches were introduced in the late 1950s, with some replaced by Mark IIs in the early 80s. A major change came in the late 1980s, when class 156 diesel multiple units replaced the loco hauled trains. A few of the latter remained for summer services until the early 1990s. By that time, the extensive parcels traffic which had lasted well into the 1970s had disappeared completely. Class 158s have operated the services since the mid-1990s. A dedicated fleet is maintained at Inverness; internally they have been refitted to place most seats by windows and provide additional accommodation for bicycles and luggage.

Special trains of course have always featured on the line but in the past they were organised for local events. For the last forty years there has been an increasing number of specials bringing tourists to the area and railway enthusiasts to the line. The luxury *Royal Scotsman* has travelled over the line; specials have also been operated to take south groups of cyclists who were brave enough to make the Land's End to John o'Groats run. Journeys on service trains are now incorporated into the itineraries of some coach tours.

While Type 2 diesels took over most of the workings north of Inverness, some Type 1s were also allocated to the area and used on freight trains. D8033 arrives at Dingwall in the 1960s. (John Roake collection)

When the Ness bridge at Inverness was washed away in 1989, several wagons were stranded and had to be taken south by road. Invergordon was a suitable place to transfer the wagons from rail to road.

(J L Stevenson)

Passengers entering Invergordon passed under this decorative arch which led directly on to the up platform. The buildings flanked this on both sides. In recent years, an attractive series of tromp d'oeil paintings, have brightened up the station, seen here in 2009 when the finial above the entrance had been damaged. Examples of the paintings are shown on page 65. Efforts have been made at other stations to find new uses for them. *(Keith Fenwick)*

Only a limited number of freight trains have operated north of Inverness in recent years. Some traffic, such as pipes for the oil industry, have naturally been for limited periods. One regular train has been the weekly oil tanks to the depot at Lairg. On 4th October 2010, 67007 crosses the modern Ness Viaduct at Inverness with the northbound working. *(Sandy Colley)*

Today and the Future

Although railway operation passed away from state control in the 1990s, the franchise system and the heavy operational subsidy necessary to keep the Far North line open means that the state retains considerable influence over the service provided. Since devolution, this has been exercised from Edinburgh through Transport Scotland, whose policies have supported rail development within the constraints of the funds available.

The Highlands and Islands Transport Partnership (HITRANS) has been set up as a statutory regional transport partnership for the Highland region plus the Western Isles, Orkney, Moray and most of Argyll and Bute. It works with all the public bodies to improve transport services and infrastructure in the north of Scotland and on routes to the Highlands and Islands. HITRANS and its predecessor, often spurred on by the voluntary Friends of the Far North Line, have promoted the additional services introduced over the last few years which mean that there are now more trains than ever before. This is partly to promote tourism but just as much to ensure that all residents have access to health and educational facilities and to relieve ever increasing congestion around the rapidly developing Inverness area. HITRANS has also been actively promoting the use of the line by freight trains, but this is frustrated by the limited amount of traffic on offer. There have been contracts for specific traffic for a few months but no long-term traffic flows which would provide the basis for sustained development. With the current level of passenger service, the number of crossing points also limits the running of additional freight or special passenger trains.

There is little opportunity for further substantial reduction in the cost of operating the line. The number of people employed at stations had been gradually reduced as goods and parcels traffic declined and passengers bought their tickets on the train. Most stations became completely unstaffed after radio signalling was introduced and now only Dingwall is staffed and only for part of the day. Track maintenance has been mechanised and is now covered by one gang.

The only way the subsidy can now be reduced is through increased use; here the franchise operator, First ScotRail, has been active with various fare deals, improvements to the rolling stock used and the encouragement of the use of trains for tourist parties. Local support from Friends of the Kyle Line and Friends of the Far North Line has added to the enjoyment of these journeys. This has achieved such success that some trains are now full to standing in summer, so more stock is needed but that in turn requires more investment.

The future of the line is today in the hands of the politicians. At present its prospects appear as bright as they ever have been. Transport needs have changed, particularly over the last half century and the railway has shown that it can adapt.

Not only was the third Duke of Sutherland much involved in the building of the lines north of Inverness, he also owned his own locomotive and made an agreement with the Highland Railway in 1871 that he could use it on the line to Inverness. The fourth Duke obtained a new engine, named Dunrobin, *in 1895 designed by David Jones and a small saloon to run with it. The cab was luxuriously fitted out so that he could drive the locomotive and entertain guests on the footplate. He also owned a large saloon for his journeys south from Inverness. This was not normally used north of there, but it is seen behind the 0-4-4 tank at Inverness on 10th September 1921 when it was waiting to take the Prince of Wales and Duke of Rothesay (later Edward VIII and George VI respectively) to Dunrobin Castle.* Dunrobin *was purchased from the Duke in the late 1940s and spent many years at Dymchurch in Kent and then in British Columbia, Canada. It is now being restored for use at Beamish Musuem, Co Durham, so we may soon once again see a locomotive designed at Lochgorm in operation. (HRS collection)*

When single line tokens were in use, exchange apparatus, such as this at Muir of Ord, was provided as manual exchange at speed was dangerous. Sometimes all did not go well as in this case in 1969 when the token being dropped can be seen flying in the air. At Muir of Ord, the tablet for the next section was picked up at the south box. (Keith Fenwick)

Bibliography and Sources

Original sources :

Minutes of the Inverness & Ross-shire, Inverness & Nairn, Inverness & Aberdeen Junction and Highland Railways in National Records of Scotland, General Register House, Edinburgh.

Contemporary newspapers - *Inverness Courier, Banffshire Journal.*

Published works consulted or containing further reading :

British Railways and the Great War, Edwin A Pratt, Selwyn & Blount.

Cromarty & Dingwall Light Railway, Eric H Malcolm, Cromarty Courthouse, 1993, ISBN 1 89841602 8.

Dingwall Canal, by Kenneth R Clew, Dingwall Museum.

Highland Railway, David Ross, Stenlake Publishing, 2010, ISBN 9781840334975.

Highland Railway, O S Nock, Ian Allan, 1965.

Highland Railway Albums, Volumes 1 and 2, Anthony J Lambert, Ian Allan, 1974, ISBN 071100532X and 1978, ISBN 0711008779, respectively.

Highland Railway, Its Constituents and Successors, Stephenson Locomotive Society, 1955.

Highland Railway Locomotives, Books 1 and 2, Cormack and Stevenson, RCTS, 1988, ISBN 0 90115 64 9 and ISBN 0 901115 72 X.

Highland Railway : People and Places, Neil T Sinclair, Breedon Books, 2005, ISBN 1 85983 453 1.

Highland Railway Journal, Highland Railway Society, various issues.

History of the Highland Railway, by H.A. Vallance, updated by Clinker and Lambert as *The Highland Railway,* House of Lochar, ISBN 1 899863 07 9.

LMS Engine Sheds, Volume 6, Hawkins, Reeve and Stevenson, Irwell Press 1989, ISBN 1 871608 04X.

Lost Stations on the Far North Line, Keith Fenwick, Neil T Sinclair and Richard Ardern, Highland Railway Society, 2010, ISBN 978095454854 4.

Rails to Wick & Thurso, David McConnell, 1990, ISBN 0 9513358 7 1.

Regional History of the Railways of Great Britain, Volume 15, North of Scotland, John Thomas and David Turnock, David St John Thomas, ISBN 0946537 03 8.

Skye Railway, John Thomas, House of Lochar, ISBN 0 946537 48 8.

Companion Volumes by the Highland Railway Society celebrating 150th Anniversaries

Inverness & Aberdeen Junction Railway, Keith Fenwick and Neil T Sinclair, 2008, ISBN 978 9054548537.

Inverness & Nairn Railway, Keith Fenwick, 2005, ISBN 978 0954548513.

Perth & Dunkeld Railway, Keith Fenwick and Neil T Sinclair, 2006, ISBN 0-954548523.

Other Highland Railway Society Publications

Pioneers of the Highland Tracks, William and Murdoch Paterson, A Biography of two Railway Engineers, Anne-Mary Paterson, 2010. ISBN 978 095454855 1.

Aberfeldy's Railway, C J Stewart, 2012. ISBN 978 095454856 8.

Directors, Dilemmas and Debt, Peter Fletcher, published jointly by the Highland Railway Society and the Great North of Scotland Railway Association, 2010. ISBN 978 090234323 8.

Postcards were very popular in late Victorian and Edwardian days so the Highland Railway published sets for sale at each station. Usually these showed nearby scenes but sometimes they featured stations or trains. This one of Invergordon shows a double-headed southbound train waiting to depart. The open wagon between the locomotives and carriages could have been used to carry fish. The goods yard and harbour branch were to the right. *(John Roake collection)*

THE HIGHLAND RAILWAY SOCIETY

The Highland Railway Society caters for all those interested in the varied aspects of the railway, including its predecessors and its successors to the present day.

An illustrated quarterly Journal is distributed to members and contains a wide variety of articles and information. Members queries are a regular feature and details of new books, videos and models of interest are reported. The Society's publications include a series of books commemorating the 150th anniversaries of the opening of various sections of the system.

Meetings are held in both Scotland and England. An Annual Gathering is held each September and includes a full day of talks, films, etc., as well as an opportunity to meet fellow members.

The Society has Library, Photographic and Drawing collections which are available to members. Copies of drawings are available for purchase. Modellers are well catered for. Complete kits are produced in limited runs. Specially commissioned modelling components such as axle boxes, buffers and springs are available, plus a comprehensive set of transfers to enable any Highland loco to be named.

Membership details can be found on the our website at www.hrsoc.org.uk.